C000270663

CALLINGTON R₄

BERE ALSTON-CALSTOCK-CAL⸺

Roger Crombleholme • Bryan Gibson
Douglas Stuckey • Charles Whetmath

An account of the East Cornwall Mineral Railway and the Southern Railway's branch-line from Bere Alston to Callington from its inception as part of the Plymouth Devonport & South Western Junction Railway, together with notes on the mines and shipping whose stories are inseparably linked with the history of these railways..

Contents

	Introduction	3
1	Mining	5
2	Shipping	9
3	The First Railway at Calstock	11
4	Bere Alston & Calstock Railway	15
5	The Line is Completed	17
6	Grouping and Nationalisation	23
7	The Gunnislake Branch	27
8	The Route Described	29
9	Locomotives	33
10	Intruders	39
11	Operating the East Cornwall Mineral	41
	Appendix 1 – Principal Dimensions of Locomotives	44
	Appendix 2 – Loads of Trains	45
	Appendix 3 – Tickets	46
	Appendix 4 – Timetables	47
	Appendix 5 – Coach Service	52
	Station Plans	54
	Acknowledgements	55

First published 1967
Second Edition 1985
Third Edition 1997

FORGE BOOKS
55 Brookside,
Wokingham,
Berks RG41 2ST

EAST CORNWALL MINERAL . . .

The foot of the incline at Calstock. Loaded coal truck ascending from the Quay while horse and driver rest.

. . . TO BRITISH RAIL

Six car DMU rail tour on Calstock viaduct, 1979.

Introduction

The East Cornwall Mineral Railway opened on 8th May 1972, approximately 125 years before the appearance of this third edition of our booklet. It was the narrow (3ft 6 in) gauge predecessor of the standard gauge railway from Bere Alston to Callington engineered by the ubiquitous Colonel H.F. Stephens. Why trains still run here when most of the once extensive Southern Railway in the West has disappeared beneath brick and willow herb, tarmac and nettles, is part of an entirely absorbing story.

The Tamar river valley to the north of Plymouth is singularly beautiful, and has remained down the the present, in many places, singularly inaccessible. For this reason the railway discussed in these pages is not merely a convenient alternative to road transport but for some communities their sole reasonably direct passage to Plymouth, which is their natural focus for business and pleasure. These are quiet centres of a fertile warm humidity, home to relaxed Devon and Cornwall folk and, increasingly, the commuters who value a tranquil leisure environment after work. But their present day attractive greening conceals a history of prolonged mining activity and hectic maritime business on the slow-sliding waters.

"Few rivers wind so strangely as the Tamar" wrote Arthur Norway in the 1919 edition of *Highways and Byways in Devon and Cornwall.* "Not far above Cotehele" (splendid old 16th century mansion now a National Trust property) "one passes on the left hand the little town of Calstock, famed for its strawberries, a struggling hillside village of no great picturesqueness, but possessing a fine church on the summit of the ridge . . . the scenery around has grown so singularly grand as to claim one's whole attention."

"A few mines which deface and scar the river's bank do but increase the glow and colour of the forest by its contrast with their grimy galleries and black heaps of poisonous arsenic dust."

One must not be totally seduced by a 'strawberries and cream' vision of Calstock in the nineteenth century. Until late in the century its social and sanitary arrangements were of a remarkably low order, and many of its people tended to relieve the burden of living without proper drains or running water and consequent chronic ill-health, by a resort to drunkenness in which visiting boat trippers often participated. An inspecting medical officer of health reported in May 1854: 'a picture of filthiness such as could scarcely be equalled in the rude hamlets of savage life.'

Between the steep, wooded slopes of the Tamar and the small but ancient town of Callington lies the eminence of Kit Hill, a fine 1,000 feet high viewpoint crowned with a preserved ornate mine chimney. Callington station was inconveniently situated beyond Kit Hill at Kelly Bray, a plodding full-mile from the town. In 1966, amid the heavy railway prunings of the sixties, the Callington end of the branch was lopped off leaving a new terminal point at Gunnislake. Indeed, the Callington townsfolk understandably already relied on their cars or Western National for their journeys.

It is extremely fortunate that this railway survives not merely as essential local transport but as one of the most scenic and appealing rail journeys in the south west, reaching its most spectacular where the little train tip-toes on to the lofty and elegant Calstock viaduct, with a beautiful riverine panorama below. Local authorities and British Rail, in its various guises, down to the present owners, Wales and West Railway, have made creditable efforts to publicise the line and most recently, Sundays and Bank Holidays in summer have seen a number of subsidised tourist bus services connecting with trains at Gunnislake, to take visitors to Morwellham, Dartmoor and other popular destinations normally difficult of access by public transport, particularly at week-ends and holidays.

The railways of which this is the story were not initially concerned with the carriage of the fertilisers, strawberries and broccoli, and the farmers and labourers of the agricultural community, although these services dominated the early 20th century, but with that copper, tin and 'poisonous arsenic' and the coal to drive the machines which would extract the ore from this famously – world famously – mineral-rich soil. This was the *raison d'etre* of the East Cornwall Mineral Railway and in its early days of the standard line from Bere Alston and it seems most useful to begin with a look at the ancient mines of the area and the ships which originally served them.

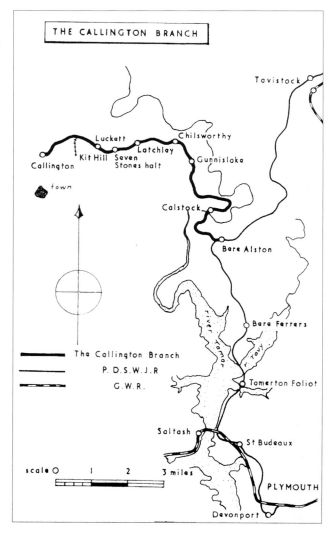

1 – Mining

Kelly Bray, Kit Hill, Hingston Down, Calstock and Bere Alston together constitute a varied mining area which was worked from time immemorial. A myriad investors, engineers, and companies have sought wealth in the district, sometimes with more enthusiasm and power of persuasion than technical ability, care and patience or capital. The proliferation of unco-ordinated independent operations meant that frequently when one was closed as a failure pumping ceased and nearby successful workings were flooded and had to be abandoned. Not for nothing were the share-holders of these undertakings usually officially styled "The Adventurers".

As long ago as the days of Charles I and II the silver-tongued Thomas Bushell, "the superlative Prodigall", whipped up enthusiasm for working on Kit Hill with the new technique of horizontal drainage adits. The well-known proverb –
"Hingston Down well-y-wrought
Is worth London town dear-y-bought"
was used as a sort of sales slogan. Bushell reported to his mentor Lord Bacon: "Hingston Down within longitude east and west five miles, with millions of shafts that have been visibly sunk upon several lodes of metal by the Romans, Danes, Saxons, Jews and Britons, and is in breadth 700 fathoms at the basis lying north and south, as well as in depth 200 fathoms from the Beacon perpendicular to the centre of that adit now intended." Hingston Down was, too, the traditional meeting place of the joint stannary parliament for Devon and Cornwall. Many were to find rich ore and their fortunes then and later, but the bonanza years were limited and the glory and the mining families have all departed.

In 1899, W. F. Wilkinson writing of the Holmbush, Redmoor and Kelly Bray mines, the group around the Callington terminus of the ECMR stated: "with regard to their mineral wealth it has been calculated that they have produced ores of copper, tin, lead, silver and arsenic to the value of about half a million sterling. It was at these mines that experiments with pumping engines were being carried out in the early days when waterworks for London and other large cities were being constructed and doubtless the study of the Holmbush engine led to many improvements in the use of steam."

One or other of these three mines was usually working continuously during the period between 1796 and 1892 and there have been later short-term development operations in 1907-1914, the 1930s and 1941-43.

It was not until 1845 that mine-owners were compelled to keep correct plans of the workings and to deposit them with the Home Office when work was suspended. Even then the plans were often primitive, inaccurate and to a number of different and peculiar scales, so resumption of work was fraught with some danger.

The 80ft chimney stack on the crown of the granite outcrop of Kit Hill itself marks the remains of Kit Hill Great Consols, an undertaking which continued well into the 20th century yielding £15,000 of tin in the best years of 1902-03. The East Kithill and South Kithill tin mines were less important concerns: during the 1914-18 war mineral shortages led to a good deal of surface prospecting and adit driving at East Kithill and an aerial ropeway operated by 4 men and 4 boys carried up to 20 tons of material every hour to Hingston

Down 2½ miles away. On the summit of Kit Hill was erected the only windmill used for drainage power in the West.

One of the most extensively equipped and most recently worked of the area's mines was New Consols at Luckett. In the early 1870s when 112 fathoms deep, New Consols had "two pumping engines of 80in and 50in . . . together with a 50ft x 4ft 6in water wheel . . . a 24in steam whim, two other water wheel whims and several horse whims; a 36in engine operating 36 head of stamps: a 28in crusher plus a smaller 12in crusher . . . large dressing floors were laid out with no less than seven calciners and ten reverbatory furnaces, together with over a mile of flues and arsenic chambers . . ." and so on. As might have been expected this lavish outlay inhibited profitable operation.

Arsenic was an important product here too, and there was trouble with complaints that the fumes were injuring the countryside and the people. Sidings to serve Luckett were provided at Monks Corner (Luckett Station) on the ECMR but a projected inclined tramway to New Consols was never constructed. In 1947 after 70 years of idleness the mine was reopened with American capital and employed as many as 160 men but the enterprise was a failure and by 1954 all was over.

On Hingston Down itself were Prince of Wales Mine on the southern slopes (copper and a smaller quantity of tin) and Hingston Down Consols at the summit with the largest output (64,440 tons of copper ore in the period 1850-82) of any mine in the area served by the ECMR. At the peak period in the 1860s the HDC employed 225 people. The main workings were 172 fathoms deep, this was deeper than most as the tough granite offered formidable resistance to boring and blasting.

In the area of Gunnislake and Calstock were Gunnislake, Gunnislake Clitters, Drakewalls, Wheal Edward, Wheal Arthur, Cotehele Consols and Calstock Consols mines. Gunnislake was the oldest of the Tamar-side copper mines and was working in the 18th century. In later days it was known as "Old Gunnislake" to distinguish it from Gunnislake Clitters which was perched on a steep slope above the Tamar. Drainage of the latter was a comparatively simple matter by means of adits driven from river level. At the end of its career in 1919 Clitters was worked by the Duchy of Cornwall. Prior to the construction of the ECMR a tramroad had been built to convey ore to wharves at the head of the Tamar navigation at Gunnislake.

Drakewalls was primarily a tin producer and was originally worked in a long "gunnis" or open cutting. After the introduction of steam stamps in the late 1860s there was a successful period of operation of seventeen years during which £218,000 of black tin was sold. In 1870 340 hands were employed. At the head of the ECMR incline, Calstock Consols, was not a profitable copper mine but at the end of the 19th century considerable quantities of mispickel (arsenic) were raised.

After the traffic in metal ores had practically ceased the wagon lift at Calstock between the railway and the quays was kept open for the shipment of local bricks and granite.

Value of Mineral Produce
from Holmbush, Kelly Bray and Redmoor Mines 1874-92

	1874-78	1880-88	1889-92	TOTAL
	£	£	£	1876-92
Arsenic ore	18,663	71,139	27.687	117,489
Copper ore	3,120	10,973	5,677	19,770
Lead ore	———	1,250	———	1,250
Tin ore	168	1,296	19,291	20,755
Wolfram ore	———	30	———	30
				159,294

Left: Stamps Engine at Wheal Martha.

Bottom: Drakewalls Mine looking South East, December 1934.

Two pictures of Calstock Viaduct under construction. There was some difficulty in finding the foundation for the pillar where the crane is fixed in the top photograph. The lower photograph shows the quay sidings of the East Cornwall Mineral Railway.

2 – Shipping

The Tamar has been navigable up to Morwellham since the 12th century but the broad, twisting, slow-sliding waters of the Tamar and Tavy are desolate today above Plymouth. The myriad ferries which are shown on quite recent ordnance surveys have disappeared; road bridges are practically non-existent and for places like Bere Alston and Gunnislake rail is still a regular conveyance for a greater part of the population than places less isolated.

However, before the railway came the waterways were bustling with shipping, pleasure steamers taking parties for strawberry and cream teas at Calstock (it is interesting that mining and tourism were able to flourish side-by-side as many Cornishmen hope and believe they could again now), schooners and steamships with manure and coal for the mines or returning with cargoes of ore for Wales (the terminus of the ECMR was at Williams Quay, leased as ore and coal yards by Vivian & Sons, the Swansea smelters and coal factors) or Liverpool. At the quays ships were built and operated by local people and there was an attractive maritime business to be seen at places where today one can sit for an hour or two and view nothing alive save a handful of gulls and a single lazy cormorant.

Calstock itself where the river was "the only means of transport" had a particular variety of craft. Market boats such as the "Ariel" and "Empress" carried passengers to Plymouth every day towards the end of the 19th century and brought back tourists as far as Weir Head. There were no commercial refreshment places in Calstock but housewives in stiff white aprons waited to take parties to their cottages for tea. On Tuesdays, Thursdays and Saturdays produce was carried to and from Plymouth.

For local cargoes sailing barges were used intensively. At the end of the 19th century a barge of this type which carried a crew of two, cost about £400. These barges carried between 40 and 70 tons apiece and difficult turns were negotiated with the assistance of two oars or sweeps about 20ft in length. In shallow water two huge punting poles were brought into use. Trains of three or four barges or schooners were often towed to Calstock by steam paddle tugs.

Shipbuilding was carried on by the Calstock & Devonport Steam Packet Company, and Lang & Co., and on the Devon bank by the Amalgamated Devon & Cornwall Steam Packet Co., and Goss & Sons by the Ashburton Hotel. Eighty years ago there were approximately 20 cargo ships on the river. Captain Samuells owned the "Naiad", the "Jacinte", "Devonport" and "Ticino": others were jointly owned by the captain of the vessel and members of the local community. A Calstock-built ship might average between 150 and 300 tons carrying capacity. In addition to the ore from the ECMR, granite and brick were shipped from the Quay. Then "all along the river bank from Ashburton Hotel at the west end of Calstock to the New Bridge at Gunnislake" could be heard the "rattle of windlass, weighing of anchor and the vibrating chatter of old winches."

The ferries on the Tamar were usually operated by local people for the benefit of local travellers, and their existence came and went without much notice from the outside world – and often escaped the eyes of the Ordnance Survey cartographers. There were passages at Weir Head, Gawton, Calstock, Cotehele, Cargreen and elsewhere – most disappeared between the wars, after the mine chimneys had gone cold – Cargreen went about 1920,

Halton Quay in 1926, and Calstock as late as 1967. At the end of the 18th century the Tamar Manure Navigation undertook to make the river navigable from Morwellham as far as Tamerton Bridge, but, in the event, only 2½ miles as far as Newbridge (Gunnislake) was completed and this itself closed by 1929.

Two companies currently provide summer trips to Calstock, Plymouth Boat Cruises (successors to Millbrook Steamboat Company which once operated bus services to Kingsand and Cawsand from its Millbrook base) and Tamar Cruising (proprietors of the Cremyll Ferry) who also offer trips to Morwellham. Plymouth to Calstock and back is a 4 hour cruise and fares are £4 single and £6 return. In the 1980s combined rail/river tickets could be obtained from Plymouth to Calstock at an adult fare of £2.60.

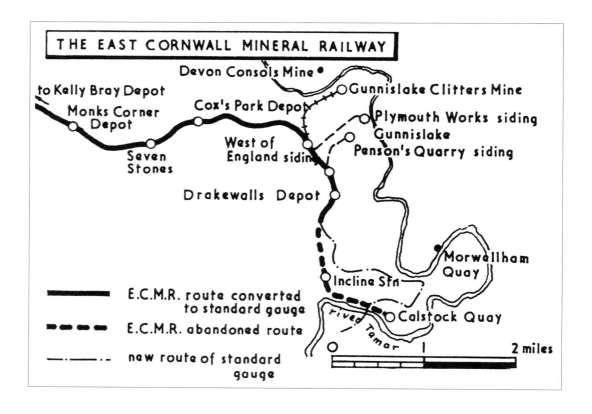

THE EAST CORNWALL MINERAL RAILWAY

3 – The First Railway at Calstock

Mining activity in the Callington and Gunnislake area reached its zenith in the middle of the nineteenth century. It was necessary for all the coal required by the mines, and ore for shipment, to be transported to and from Calstock Quay. Calstock is situated on the steep sides of the Tamar Valley, but most of the mines and quarries were on the high ground to the west, and it was very expensive and hazardous to carry the traffic by road. By the early 1860s the volume of traffic had become so great that a railway was planned to connect Calstock with Callington, seven miles distant. The Tamar, Kit Hill and Callington Railway Company Limited was formed under the provisions of the Companies Act, 1862, and the first sod was cut at Kelly Quay, Calstock, on 26th November 1863. The prospectus was issued in January 1864; the capital was to be £60,000 in £10 shares. The "Cornish & Devon Post" for 9th January 1864 reported that "much mineral traffic is anticipated . . . as at present mines have to pay 1s per ton cartage. Construction has already begun at Kelly Quay, the inclined plane, quays, engine works, stores, etc., of the Tamar Coal, Manure & General Merchandise Company have been obtained on equitable terms". The proprietors of the latter company were among the directors of the railway. The inclined plane referred to was used for the haulage of coal up the valley side. The company soon encountered difficulties, and it was necessary to obtain an Act of Parliament, which received the Royal Assent on 29th July 1864. This reformed the company (without limited liability) with an authorised capital of £70,000. In November 1864 the Calstock Railway announced its intention to seek powers to build a railway from the TKH&CR at the "Commercial Wharf", Calstock across the Tamar to Hatches Mill in the parish to Buckland Monachorum, presumably with the intention of serving Devon Great Consols Mine.

In 1865 an Act of Parliament was obtained authorising the Saltash & Callington Railway, which was to be a broad gauge branch of the Cornwall Railway, partially following the route of an earlier abortive scheme, the Plymouth & North Cornwall Railway of 1845. The TKH&CR had been authorised as a standard gauge line and to enable connection to be made with the Saltash & Callington a further Act was obtained in 1866 permitting the use of the broad gauge; it was stipulated that the gauge was to be mixed should connection be made with any standard gauge line in the future. Although considerable progress had been made with the construction of the TKH&CR the financial crisis of 1866 prevented its completion, and no work was undertaken on the Saltash & Callington.

The local mines were facing growing competition from imported ores, exacerbated by the poor local transport facilities; to meet the demand it was decided to promote a second railway from Calstock to Callington, using the partially completed works of the TKH&CR. As the Callington & Calstock Railway, this was authorised by an Act of 9th August 1869. The authorised capital was £60,000, and the first directors were Arthur Chandler, Thomas Vivian Gurney and James Rhodes. The line was to be 7 miles, 7 furlongs 2 chains long, in three sections: Callington - Top of Incline 7 miles 2 chains, Incline 3 furlongs 3 chains, Quay 3 furlongs 7 chains. The Act permitted any gauge between 3ft and 4ft 8½in, and 3ft 6in was adopted. Unlike the TKH&CR passengers were not allowed to be carried. Construction started almost immediately and proceeded steadily. A further Act was obtained on 25th May 1871 authorising a change of name to the East Cornwall Mineral Railway; and abandonment of part of the route at Callington. The line was officially opened throughout on 8th May 1872. Two steam locomotives were purchased for use on the upper section, and horses were employed on the Quay. The incline was worked by a 14 hp stationary engine.

Proposed extensions

The line was an immediate success, being a great improvement on the previous packhorse transport, and it was decided to extend the line to join the main railway system. At this time the nearest main line railways were the Cornwall Railway from Plymouth to Truro, and the Tavistock & Launceston branch of the South Devon Railway, both broad gauge associates of the GWR. However, on 12th October 1874, the Devon & Cornwall Railway, which was a standard gauge line worked by the London & South Western Railway, extended its line from Okehampton to Lidford,* on the Launceston line of the South Devon. This latter line was converted to mixed gauge in 1876. In the same year the ECMR presented a bill to Parliament for a standard gauge extension, 7 miles 1 furlong 1 chain in length from the top of the Incline at Calstock to join the Tavistock & South Devon Railway at Tavistock; with a branch 1 mile 1 furlong 8 chains from Goaten Farm to Morwellham Quay, whence there was already a tramway to the famous Devon Great Consols Mine. The Royal Assent was given on 15th August 1876; under this Act the ECMR was obliged to alter the existing line to standard gauge before the extension was completed, and to make working arrangements with the LSWR. The extension was to be financed by separate "Extension" shares; the authorised capital for the extension was £200,000, and separate accounts were to be kept for the two sections, although the gauge conversion could be financed by the new capital. The previous speed limit of 16mph was to be abolished, and the carrying of passengers permitted. Unfortunately the company was unable to raise any of the capital, and it was necessary to obtain a further Act on 3rd July 1879 repealing the 1876 Act in its entirety.

Shortly afterwards a Devon & Cornwall Central Railway was formed to promote an extension of the standard gauge into Cornwall. The D&CCR introduced a Bill in the 1882 Parliamentary Session for a line from Lidford to Calstock, whence the ECMR was to be used to Callington. Branches were proposed from Lamerton to Mary Tavy (making a triangular junction with the Tavistock & Launceston line) and from near Kelly Bray to "opposite the County Police Station" in Callington. The authorised capital was £270,000 and the estimated cost £187,607 7s 6d. It was proposed to erect stations at Collacombe Down (for Milton Abbot and Lamerton), Devon Great Consols Mine, Gunnislake and Callington. The River Tamar was to be crossed by a high level bridge 800 yards long and with a maximum height of 230ft. Opposition came from the GWR and the promoters of the Tavistock & Gunnislake Railway, also before Parliament, which was to tunnel Morwell Down, cross the Tamar on a bridge only 87ft high to terminate at a station in Gunnislake about a mile below the ECMR depot at Drakewalls. The protagonists of this scheme claimed that by avoiding Tavistock the D&CCR was ignoring local needs; D&CCR supporters claimed that a connection between the ECMR and the D&CCR would assist the mineowners, as cheaper fuel would enable them to compete with foreign producers. Benjamin Van Tromp, Solicitor to the ECMR, stated that his company was dissatisfied with the inadequate service it could offer and welcomed a connection with the main line. On 10th May 1882 the House of Lords rejected the Tavistock & Gunnislake in favour of the D&CCR scheme, which in due course received the Royal Assent. The Act included an agreement whereby the

* Old Spelling

*The abandoned incline station in 1962, showing the engine shed (left) and the winding hut (right).
The tracks formed a loop round the water tower to the head of the incline immediately beyond.*

D&CCR would purchase the ECMR and re-equip it as a main line railway. A special meeting of ECMR Shareholders on 6th June 1882 approved the sale of their line.

As with most of the previous schemes for railways in the district, it proved difficult to raise the necessary capital, only 572 of the 27,000 authorised shares being taken up. Yet another scheme was submitted to Parliament in 1883, by the Plymouth, Devonport & South Western Junction Railway, for a railway from Lidford through Tavistock and Bere Alston to join the LSWR at Devonport (King's Road) station, with a branch to join the ECMR at Calstock. The Bill, which received the Royal Assent on 25th August 1883, included powers to make agreements to acquire the D&CCR and all its obligations (including purchase of the ECMR). In the next session a further Act was obtained on 7th August 1884 confirming the agreement with the D&CCR, though not until the ECMR had forced the insertion of a clause requiring the PDSWJR to purchase it within one year of the opening of the line from Lidford to Devonport. This was confirmed by a further PDSWJR Act obtained on 19th July 1887; the purchase price was fixed at £62,500 and the PDSWJR was to pay interest at 5%, if payment was not made. The final payment was of £48,250 in ordinary PDSWJR shares and £21,500 in cash.

At length the PDSWJR main line was complete and ready for opening, which took place on 2nd June 1890. The ECMR was duly taken over on 1st June 1891, but the actual purchase was not completed until 4th January 1894.

In the last years of the ECMR, in 1891, it suffered with the rest of the west country one of the most violent storms of all time. For three or four days in early March it raged and the river valley around Cotehele was stripped of trees by winds and enormous weights of snow;

the old house itself was damaged and 100,000 cu ft of timber had fallen. A party of Cornish miners led by ECMR general manager, Captain William Sowden successfully fought through to Kelly Bray clearing the line as they went. Curiously, in the great desert of devastation close to Calstock all the mine chimneys survived the tempest.

When the ECMR was wound up its Secretary was D. Amey. At its opening in 1872 the General Manager was T. F. Mitchell, and the Accountant, C. Grant Smith. In 1874 the latter became General Manager, the separate post of Accountant being abolished. He was succeeded by C. H. Reynolds in 1880. On the latter's resignation in 1883 Captain W. Sowden was appointed to the post, and he continued as manager under the PDSWJR until 1908. To run the ECMR the PDSWJR formed a committee which originally comprised Messrs Venning, Church and J. W. Burchell, the Secretary.

Although the PDSWJR intended to make the connection to the ECMR as soon as possible, this had to be deferred because of the difficulty of raising capital. The powers for the connection expired in November 1897 and were not renewed immediately.

The Callington Light Railway

Meanwhile public pressure for the railway was growing, and there was a threat of competition for in 1895 at a public meeting in Callington details were announced of a proposed new line from Saltash to Callington. The "Cornish & Devon Post" reported that: "the proposed junction shall be close to Saltash station, the line passing under St Stephen's Road. There will be a level crossing at Burraton, with a stopping place at Notter, the line being then continued to St Mellion, passing under the main road near Viverdon Down. Somewhere between St Mellion and St Dominick stopping places will be arranged for those villages. Passing under the main Callington and Tavistock road it would enter from the north side of the town. There will be some rather heavy gradients, averaging 1 in 50. It is anticipated that the outside cost including the necessary land would be £60,000. Mr P. W. Meik, the consulting engineer, did not consider it advisable to go in for narrow gauge . . . it would no doubt be cheaper, but the line was very short and the saving would be very small. It is the intention of the promoters if the line is successful to extend to Launceston." No further progress was made immediately, but taking advantage of the passing of the Light Railways Act in 1896 the promoters, the Light Railway Development Company, obtained the Callington Light Railway Order in 1900. The cost of the railway was estimated at £99,792. No construction was undertaken and an Order granting an extension of time was obtained in 1903. No work had been carried out when the powers were vested in the GWR in 1907. Shortly afterwards the GWR introduced a motor omnibus service between Saltash and Callington,* and although preparatory work on the railway was undertaken, and a further extension of time obtained in 1909, it was felt that the omnibus service was adequate for local needs, and the powers lapsed.

---

* A coach service between Tavistock and Liskeard via Callington operated in conjunction with the LSWR from 1876 to 1908– see Appendix 5.

4 – Bere Alston & Calstock Railway

The activities of the Light Railway Development Company had aroused the PDSWJR, and in March 1898 the Secretary was instructed to investigate the possibility of constructing a railway "on the East Cornwall" gauge from Bere Alston to Calstock. It was found that this would be a workable proposition, and it was agreed to apply to the Light Railway Commissioners for an Order, subject to agreement with the Earl of Mount Edgcumbe regarding the route over his land. The Bere Alston & Calstock Light Railway Order was confirmed by the Board of Trade on 12th July 1900. It was for a line 4 miles 1 furlong 8.15 chains in length from Bere Alston to a junction with the ECMR near Calstock. The estimated cost of construction was £74,014; this was high because it was necessary to cross the Tamar on a viaduct 120ft high. The LRO gave authority for the viaduct to be considered equal to three miles for charging purposes. The authorised gauge was 3ft 6ins, and the Order permitted the working of the existing ECMR from the junction with the BAC to Kelly Bray as a light railway, and passengers were allowed to be carried thereon.

Little progress followed, and for some time there was difficulty in raising the necessary money, but eventually agreement was reached with the LSWR whereby the latter company was to take up the capital providing this was issued as 3% guaranteed stock secured on the entire undertakings of the PDSWJR. In the autumn of 1901 a bill was presented to Parliament to enable the BAC (including the ECMR) to be constituted as a separate company, with a capital of £135,000, within the PDSWJR. This received the Royal Assent on 23rd June 1902. Although the main line of the PDSWJR was leased to, and worked by, the LSWR, it was decided that it would continue to work the ECMR and BAC on its own account.

Messrs Galbraith & Church had been appointed Engineers for the construction of the BAC, and later Colonel H. F. Stephens, the well known light railway protagonist, was appointed Associate Engineer. In 1902 Messrs Galbraith & Church had been instructed to invite tenders, and to stake out the line. Before the contractors had been appointed it was necessary to apply for an Order granting an extension of time. In August 1904 the directors agreed to raise the Secretary's salary from £250 to £500 while the BAC was being constructed. The following year application was made for an amending Light Railway Order permitting the standard gauge to be employed; no local enquiry was necessary as it was practically unopposed and the Board of Trade approved the Order on 12th October 1905. The 3ft 6in gauge was to be retained to serve the Gunnislake Quarries for as long as was necessary. Colonel Stephens was appointed engineer responsible for converting the ECMR section to standard gauge, under the supervision of the Manager of the ECMR, Captain Sowden: Messrs Galbraith & Church were in charge of the new construction.

In November the Secretary was authorised to purchase the "necessary number" of 4-wheeled coaches from the LSWR at £90 each, and also to enquire whether they had any suitable engines for disposal. If not, he was to consult the engineers who were to obtain estimates for new engines. It was decided that three engines would suffice, and their names and the rolling stock livery were finalised in December. The construction of the line was well under way, though difficulty in securing a foundation for No. 9 pier of the viaduct was causing delay. Col Stephens nevertheless predicted that the line would be open by July 1906, with due diligence on the part of the contractor .

In January 1906 Colonel Stephens was asked to arrange the purchase of the engines and goods rolling stock. The directors expressed their disappointment at the slow progress being made. There was considerable local pressure for the railway to be extended from Kelly Bray to Callington, but the company would only undertake this if the land were given free. Despite Colonel Stephens' optimistic claim that the line should be open by mid-1906, it was far from complete, and no work had begun on the wagon-lift at Calstock. Work proceeded very slowly and it was not until 1908 that the line was ready. Meanwhile in May 1907 the directors had considered a proposal from mine owners that the railway be extended from Kelly Bray to the Cheesewring, but although they were willing to work such a line they were not prepared to construct it. Six months later however, a special committee of the directors unanimously reported in favour of an extension from Kelly Bray to a terminus in North Hill Parish, either at Congdon's Shop or Coad's Green. Among the reasons given it was stated that (1) the GWR was staking out the Saltash & Callington line; (2) 14,240 tons of traffic passed annually from Calstock to Kelly Bray, of which only about 500 tons was for Callington, the majority being for the "northern district"; (3) the BAC was built in anticipation of traffic from this district; (4) the traffic at this end of the line was in danger because the GWR would have the shorter route to Plymouth, GWR 'buses and a goods lorry were already running from Saltash. Accordingly it was decided to apply for a Light Railway Order. After the Light Railway Commissioners had held the local enquiry and had reported favourably on the scheme, the North Hill Light Railway Order was granted by the Board of Trade on 11th February 1909. The estimated cost of the extension was £45,433.

The viaduct in 1907 with wagon lift on left of picture nearing completion.

5 – The Line is Completed

By December 1907 all the trackwork was laid, but the stations at Calstock and Gunnislake were not complete. Major Pringle of the Board of Trade carried out the official inspection of the line on 5th February 1908, and at their meeting on 14th February the directors fixed the date of opening for Monday 2nd March. Although it had been decided that there would be no opening ceremony the PDSWJR directors and other dignitaries travelled to Callington on the 12 noon train from Bere Alston. The school children at Callington were given a half-day holiday, and, headed by the Callington Band, marched to Kelly Bray, where they were regaled with buns etc. There were a public luncheon and tea, and in the evening a concert was held in the newly built hall at Kelly Bray. It was reported in the "Cornish & Devon Post" that "the powerful engines of the company and smart commodious coaches were the centre of much attraction and admiration and throughout the day a stream of moving life poured into the station . . . every train was full of passengers."

The reconstructed railway was 9 miles 50 chains long, and when it was opened there were stations at Calstock, Gunnislake (the former Drakewalls depot, ECMR), Latchley (formerly Cox's Park), Stoke Climsland (formerly Monk's Corner) and Callington Road (formerly Kelly Bray). Stoke Climsland village was a considerable distance from its station, and was actually somewhat nearer Callington Road; following complaints by the Rev. G. B. Walters of Stoke Climsland Rectory and the Stoke Climsland Parish Council the station was renamed Luckett from 1st November 1909, and at the same time Callington Road became Callington for Stoke Climsland. A halt was opened at Chilsworthy on 1st June 1909.

The reconstruction of the ECMR was so well planned that the ordinary traffic was not suspended for more than two days during the gauge conversion, and the navvies were required to work on only two Sundays. The principal feature of the new line was Calstock Viaduct; constructed of concrete blocks, it has twelve arches, each of 60ft span. The rail level is 120ft above river level. The wagon lift that was erected to provide access to the quay was one of the highest in England, the difference in levels being 113ft. It was designed by Messrs Galbraith & Church. The cage and framework of the lift were composed almost entirely of mild steel, forming strongly braced structures with ample margin of strength. The cage could hold one four wheeled open wagon, weighing laden approximately 15 tons. The motive power for raising and lowering the cage was provided by a steam boiler and powerful winding engine fixed to the top of the lift framing. Duplicate steel wire ropes were provided to raise the cage, each of these was capable of holding the load should the other have failed. The cage was held at the top platform level by a safety securing device; safety gates at both top and bottom were worked automatically by the cage so that they closed the entrance as soon as it left either level. An electric bell was operated by the cage as it approached its destination. There was a short approach of steel girders at the top, parallel with the viaduct, along which trucks were pushed. At the lower level they were hauled out of the cage on to a turntable and turned on to the sidings which ran along the quay.

The initial train service comprised four journeys throughout in each direction, and one short working between Bere Alston and Gunnislake. The volume of traffic must have exceeded expectations for early in July the 6.05pm from Bere Alston was extended to

Callington Road on Saturdays, and a late evening train was run from Callington Road to Bere Alston and back on Wednesdays and Saturdays during July and August. Only first and third class accommodation was provided. In July 1908 the LSWR was approached with a view to its leasing the branch but the PDSWJR was advised to run the branch itself, which it did until the grouping. The PDSWJR was to pay the LSWR £60 per annum for the use of Bere Alston. On Sunday 6th September a special train of two 6-wheeled and three 8-wheeled carriages was run from Plymouth to Callington, being hauled over the branch by the engine "Lord St Levan" to ascertain the practicability of avoiding a change of train at Bere Alston for excursion parties. In November it was agreed that the Secretary's salary should remain at £500, whilst Colonel Stephens' salary as manager was confirmed at £250, and he was required to attend on the line two days every week.

In March 1909 the BAC Managing Committee (formed from among the directors of the PDSWJR) visited the line and reported that passenger traffic was good, but goods and mineral traffic was poor, but in other respects the business of the line was going on well and with every sign of satisfactory and efficient management and in their view the cause of the poor goods traffic was the bad state of trade, which was practically at a standstill in the district. A steam winch had been installed at Calstock to haul trucks to and from the lift, thereby saving horse hire. It was reported that the GWR "trolly" (sic) which formerly visited Callington daily now only came once weekly. In July the conversion of twelve ECMR wagons to standard gauge for sale was approved. The tenants of property adjoining Calstock Quay applied for permission to land seaweed, but this was refused unless tolls were paid. The following February a slight improvement in traffic was noted, and the Kit Hill Granite Company restarted activities. The indefatigable Mr Venning of Callington, who frequently suggested the construction of various extensions, requested that a halt be built at Phoenix Brick Works for pleasure parties to the neighbouring Phoenix Pleasure Grounds, then very popular with Sunday School parties from Plymouth. This was approved and a halt, known as Seven Stones, was erected adjacent to the pleasure grounds, midway between Latchley and Luckett. Opened in June 1910, the halt was in use until the pleasure grounds closed in September 1917.

The Managing Committee decided in March 1910 that a Resident Manager for the Light Railway was necessary. Colonel Stephens was duly notified and was asked to act as Engineer, responsible for locomotives, permanent way and rolling stock. As after five months it had not been possible to arrange a meeting with Colonel Stephens, it was felt impracticable to have him as engineer, so the Secretary was instructed to write to him, terminating his connection with the railway from 30th June 1910. In his place Mr T. H. Gibbons was appointed Engineer and Mr S. G. Hartnell, Traffic Manager. At the same time the Traffic Office was moved from Calstock to Callington. In July 1910 it was decided to erect a carriage shed at Luckett. In the following March six coaches were sold to Colonel Stephens for £29 each, free on rail at Bere Alston. At the same time it was decided to sell the ex-ECMR saddle tank, No. 2, if a suitable price could be obtained. It, too, was eventually sold to Colonel Stephens in July 1912, for £250 less carriage, for service on the Hundred of Manhood & Selsey Tramway. In July 1911 the Traffic Manager's salary was fixed at £150, plus 6s per week canvassing allowance, and £16 rent allowance. In September the company followed the LSWR example in making an additional payment to staff who had remained on duty during recent strike troubles; a letter was sent by the staff concerned to the directors expressing their appreciation. Early in 1912 the lift man at Calstock was dispensed with, as the lift was rarely used. A coal strike caused the train service to be reduced in March. The summer produced a very poor strawberry and raspberry crop – this was a very

Opening of the new railway: A.S. Harris *heads a train across Calstock Viaduct on 2nd March, 1908.*

valuable traffic, several of the leading companies sending special canvassers to the district. In September Mr Gibbons, the engineer, died and Mr W. J. Foxlee was appointed in his stead, at a salary of 100 guineas, chargeable 50% to the Permanent Way and 50% to the Locomotive & Coaching Departments. It was decided in November to convert the Traffic Manager's Office at Callington into a stationery store, and use the station house, occupied by Ganger Ackford as the Office. At the same time the company was making fruitless attempts to find a house for Mr Hartnell.

In January 1913 Mr Foxlee presented a new plan for an extension to Callington but recommended that it be not carried out at the time owing to insufficient traffic, but suggested that arrangements be made for motor omnibuses to connect Kelly Bray with Callington and surrounding districts. At the same time a deputation was received from the County Court Leet pressing for the Callington extension to be built, but as it could not guarantee receipts the proposal was rejected as uneconomic. Shortly afterwards arrangements were made for a motor omnibus service between Kelly Bray and Callington, the railway paying a subvention of 5s per week. Later in the year it was decided not to apply for an extension of time in which to construct the North Hill extension, as the GWR had no plans for extending into the district, and it was felt that road motor transport was adequate. At this time it was also decided to remodel the layout at Callington to include a run-round, to avoid the necessity of keeping a turnover engine in steam.

The PDSWJR issued a comprehensive Time Book and Excursion Programme, costing a half-penny, containing details of the train service on the "Bere-Alston & East Cornwall line", with connections at Bere-Alston for LSWR mainline stations, and details of the many cheap fares available, including Walking Tickets from Plymouth and Devonport to various stations on the line, the passengers returning from other specified stations, and Tourist return tickets to various resorts served by the LSWR and associated companies. Tourists were exhorted to travel by the "new route" to see the "most beautiful and picturesque scenery in Cornwall", and cheap excursions were offered to Sunday Schools, Wesley Guilds, Bands of Hope etc. travelling to the Phoenix Pleasure Grounds at Seven Stones. The North Hill coach service ran each Thursday and Saturday, leaving Congdon Shop (for North Hill) at 8.35 am, to connect with the 10.2 am train from Callington station. In the reverse direction it connected with the 5.52 pm arrival at Callington on Thursdays, and the 6.29 pm on Saturdays. There was also a 'bus service between Callington station and town.

The line came under government control during the period of the first world war. In 1914 a siding was laid in at Chilsworthy to serve Hill, Westlake & Co's brickworks, the traffic from which was shipped from Calstock Quay. The following year the SS "Alexandria", owned by the Plymouth Pavilion Pier Company, caused slight damage to the fender of one of the piers of Calstock viaduct. The war caused a labour shortage and difficulty was experienced in handling the strawberry traffic. The remaining staff were caused a considerable amount of extra work: a special payment of £20 was made to Mr Hartnell for his work in preparing the accounts for the Railway Executive Committee, and Mr Burchell, the secretary, was paid an additional £100. His salary not only covered his personal remuneration but also the provision of the company's offices and an adequate and skilled staff. In December 1915 Locomotive Foreman Stewart retired and Driver Neale took his place at a "salary" of 45s per week. Assistant Driver May became driver and assistant fitter at 32s 6d and it was necessary to engage a new cleaner at 18s 6d. In June 1916 a Mr Batten took over the 'bus and goods delivery service at Callington following complaints of poor service. The following January Lt Holley, the Assistant Purchasing Officer for Government Hay Traffic, moved his office from Launceston to Callington, and Mr Hartnell arranged for him to use the Porters' Room and small store as an office, and the Luckett carriage shed was made available for drying hay. Instructions of the Railway Executive Committee had increased fares generally on 1st January 1917, but because the GWR had not increased the 'bus fare between Callington and Saltash it had become cheaper to travel to Plymouth by the GWR route, and the PDSWJR fare was reduced to the level of the GWR on the 17th March.

After the war the line had a fairly uneventful existence. In 1919 the platform at Callington was extended. There was a strike in October and only Inspector Gibbs and Driver Neale remained at work. However Mr Hartnell was able to arrange for some goods trains to run, particularly to rescue some horses stranded at Bere Alston. It was necessary to lengthen the cattle dock at Callington and alter the signal interlocking to accommodate the traffic for the Royal Cornwall Agricultural Show, which visited the town in 1920. The war had caused a considerable rise in wages; in 1913 they had totalled £2,160, but in 1920 the figure was £7,008. In the same period merchandise traffic rose from 29,410 tons to 36,202 tons. The salaries of the staff were standardised with those of the leading companies in 1921. In that year four bogie coaches were purchased from the LSWR for £800 each to replace stock which had become worn out. It was hoped to hire the coaches pending absorption by the LSWR under the Railways Act but this was dropped because the LSWR were unable to put forward a suitable scheme. The amount of compensation payable to the PDSWJR under the Railways Act was £1,126. The first proposal of the LSWR for absorption was rejected as inadequate but agreement was later reached. Unlike many small companies the PDSWJR was always able to pay a dividend: In most years the full 4½% on the preference shares, and 1¼% on the ordinary shares, though for the second half of 1921 4¾% was paid on the latter, with the assistance of the compensation money.

A. S. Harris *at Bere Alston with the 2.15pm to Callington.*

A lengthy mixed train: A.S. Harris *gets under way from Calstock with the 10.55 from Bere Alston to Callington.*

Exterior of Callington station taken just before opening of passenger services, 1907 with cover (later removed) over adjacent track.

Interior of Callington station with O2 Class 30225 in 1954.

6 – Grouping and Nationalisation

In the early days of the Southern Railway the train service differed little from that provided in 1914, except that all trains called at each station, and a Sunday service of two trains in each direction was introduced from 24th April 1924. In the late 1920s there was still local support for a northward extension of the railway. In October 1926 a meeting in Camelford Town Hall gave enthusiastic support to a scheme for a light railway from Kelly Bray to Boscastle, passing through North Hill, Altarnun, Camelford and Tintagel. The estimated cost of the 28 mile line was £250,000. Doubtless the promoters had been encouraged by the recent opening of the Torrington and Halwill line, but that proved to be the last example of lengthy railway construction in England. Owing to a decline in shipment traffic, particularly bricks, the wagon lift at Calstock was closed in September 1934, and dismantled the following month. Since then the quay has ceased to handle any commercial traffic and there is now little evidence of its former activity. By this time "A. S. Harris" had left the branch and its place was taken by an ex-LSWR "O2" class 0-4-4 tank. Callington shed had become a sub-shed of Plymouth (Friary) and it was the practice to stable there one of the 0-6-2 tanks and an "O2" for a week at a time.

The air raids on Plymouth in 1941 caused a large number of the residents to leave the city, and many found new homes in the Calstock and Gunnislake area, and travelled daily to and from work in Plymouth. This caused considerable overcrowding on branch trains; the maximum the 0-6-2 tanks were allowed to haul was six bogie coaches, and this was frequently exceeded, particularly on the 7.10pm from Bere Alston, and double heading was necessary.

The formation of British Railways in 1948 had no immediate effect on the branch, but between 1950 and 1958 it was transferred (with the other SR lines west of Exeter) to the Western Region for commercial purposes .

For many years until 1962 the passenger service remained constant, with six trains (seven on Saturdays) in each direction between Bere Alston and Callington, with one up weekday and one down Mondays to Fridays train between Bere Alston and Gunnislake only. Two of the down trains were mixed, and an additional mixed train ran between Bere Alston and Gunnislake on Wednesday, Thursday and Saturday afternoons. The complicated freight workings provided for two through services in each direction (one only on Saturdays) and two from Bere Alston to Gunnislake and back. There were also additional conditional paths for use when traffic required. On Sundays there were four passenger trains each way, one down being mixed, and a conditional freight from Gunnislake to Callington. The timetable for 1958, shown in Appendix 4, is typical of this period.

Commencing with the Summer 1962 service, the 7.57pm (SX) from Bere Alston was terminated at Gunnislake; at the same time the 9.15pm freight from Callington was discontinued and the engine returned light to Friary from Gunnislake. The Sunday service was withdrawn permanently at the end of the Summer service in the same year. In January 1963 the Western Region once again took control of the line, and all other SR lines west of Salisbury, this time for all purposes. Commencing in September of that year the service was modified so that the engine of the 7.57pm from Bere Alston to Gunnislake worked a freight forward to Callington, and the 8.03am freight from Bere Alston was withdrawn. and three engines were stabled at Callington overnight. The engines were employed on a three day cyclic roster from Exmouth Junction shed. As there was no 7.57pm from Bere Alston on Saturdays, a light engine was sent from Friary on Saturday afternoon. This was booked to double head the 3.13pm passenger train from Bere Alston but usually ran light through to Callington owing to shunting difficulties there. In the autumn of 1963 trials were conducted with Western Region "Warship", "Hymek" and D63xx class diesel locomotives with little apparent success and the Ivatt tanks remained in charge for nearly twelve months longer, until September 1964, when steam was withdrawn and the service once more completely revised. The new look did not have a very auspicious beginning for the very first train scheduled for diesel operation, the 5.30am from Callington on Monday 7th September, failed at Gunnislake and passengers had to be carried to their destinations by taxi!

By 1966 the Western Region was enthusiastically implementing the Beeching proposals for closures in the West. The former Southern network beyond Exeter was swiftly and savagely reduced. The routes to Plymouth and Barnstaple remained but Bere Alston to Okehampton was under sentence of death and the Callington branch was truncated at Gunnislake. Not even the most rabid "modernisers" could suggest how the inhabitants of Gunnislake and Calstock could cross the water to Plymouth without their trains.

The pruning took place on Saturday 5th November. The last train left Callington at 7.40 pm to the sound of detonators and fireworks. A wreath inscribed:

"In loving memory—Goodbye my friends this is the end,
We've travelled miles and miles,
I've watched your faces through the years
Show anger and tears and smiles.
Although you have criticized my timings and said I was too slow,
I've got you there and brought you back
In rain and sun and snow.
Launceston Railway Circle."

In 1964 – 11.10am Plymouth to Brighton express pauses at Bere Alston.

had been placed on the engine by Mr Lloyd Goodman (member of the Launceston Railway Circle) and Mr H. Liddle (the founder-President of the Plymouth Railway Circle). There was also a placard reading "Callington-Gunnislake line 1872, 1908-1966 – Farewell". The driver of the last train was Mr Sid. Whiteway and the guard, Mr L. Hooper.

Earlier on this bright autumn day officials of the Callington council turned up at the station for the obituaries, and a brief talk on the history of the line was given by Mr D. A. Trevanion, President of Callington Old Cornwall Society.

Trains on the last day were so well patronised that Callington ran out of tickets, despite the rival attraction of a local carnival. A good turn-out of enthusiasts from all parts was supplemented by former staff and passengers of the line who reminisced nostalgically of old times—the day when the train was stopped by caterpillars on the line, the attributes of "A. S. Harris", and lively six-coach excursions to Plymouth.

The revised service introduced on 7th November provided for eight trains each way (seven on Saturdays) on weekdays only; nearly all ran through to or from Plymouth North Road, but while the main line north from Bere Alston to Okehampton remained open there were also through services to Tavistock and Exeter Central. A substitute bus service was provided by Watson & Ford from Gunnislake station to Callington Bus Station and this ran until January 1972. It is perhaps surprising that it lasted so long as the GWR motor bus service from Callington to Saltash had replaced a relatively frequent service of horse buses; the successor Western National service was extended to Plymouth in October 1961 upon the opening of the Tamar Road Bridge immediately offering a faster service than was possible on the train via Bere Alston.

9.38am from Callington headed by an O2 crossing Calstock Viaduct 27 June 1956.

A trim Calstock station on a sunny day in 1962.

30192 at Gunnislake with the 2.20pm arrival on 27 June, 1956.

7 – The Gunnislake Branch

The Okehampton to Bere Alston section of the main line closed on 6th May 1968, the final trains running without ceremony on the previous day. With the introduction of the new timetable trains departed from Plymouth on Mondays to Saturdays at 5.15am, 7.00am, 9.10am, 11.25am, 1.15pm, 4.42pm, 6.05pm and 7.55pm, returning from Gunnislake 50/60 minutes later; some of the journeys ran a few minutes later on Summer Saturdays. There was an extra late working to and from Bere Alston departing from Plymouth at 9.40pm but this was withdrawn on 1st March 1976. Apart from this the basic service of eight return journeys has remained largely unchanged except that the first train does not run on Saturdays and since 29th May 1995 has started at 5.45am and terminated at Calstock, and the last train leaves Plymouth at 9.00pm. An experimental late train from Plymouth was tried in the early 1990s but proved unsuccessful.

The Sunday service, withdrawn from the branch proper in September 1962 and between Bere Alston and Plymouth in May 1968, was re-introduced experimentally on peak summer season Sundays in 1983 and ran until 1987. It restarted in 1990, sponsored by Devon County Council, connecting at Bere Alston with a bus link onto Dartmoor; since 1993 the railhead for the bus link has been Gunnislake and the destinations served have gradually been expanded. "Santa Specials" were a regular feature on the Sundays preceding Christmas for many years but did not run in 1996, a casualty of the fragmentation of the railways following privatisation.

Motive power since 1968 has been dominated by diesel multiple unit operation, originally using what would have been 3-car suburban units with the centre nonpowered car removed because of the severe gradients between Bere Alston and Gunnislake, or on occasion a single car unit. The prototype railbus No.140 001 made two demonstration runs on the Gunnislake branch on 3rd July 1981 and returned to Laira depot (Plymouth) in 1984 for driver training in readiness for a new fleet of class 142 railbuses which was intended to replace the ageing fleet of diesel multiple units, by then some 25 years old. The railbuses duly arrived in 1985 but unsurprisingly proved remarkably unsuccessful on the Gunnislake line and the other sharply curved and steeply graded Cornish branch lines. The long wheelbase of the four-wheeled vehicles caused considerable tyre and flange wear and the screeching as they negotiated the curves was unbearable. They were soon banished to the Manchester area where their chocolate and cream livery was an incongruous as it had been on the former Southern lines in Devon, and the original units returned.

Eventually class 150 and single car 153 Sprinter diesel multiple units arrived at Laira to replace what had by now become known as 'heritage' sets, but the older trains held sway on the Gunnislake branch until May 1992 when after a series of tests the class 150s were allowed to take over; initially the class 153 were only permitted as far as Calstock because of their extra length but they can now run all the way.

Until its closure the siding serving the Royal Naval Armament Depot at Ernesettle on the northern outskirts of Plymouth had a daily freight hauled by a class 08 diesel shunter. The weedkilling train makes its annual springtime visit between two class 20s; class 08s or 37s usually power any engineering trains with the occasional class 47 but they are prohibited beyond Bere Alston. Special locomotive hauled trains are now a rarity; one notable visit was a Merchant Navy Locomotive Society special on 16th April 1977 which produced Southern 33104 and 33106 and the sight once again of a Southern train on a former Southern line, albeit only as far as Bere Alston. On 21st December 1985 a railtour formed of a Hastings diesel electric multiple unit ran from Waterloo through to Gunnislake.

Today's travellers to Gunnislake join the train at Plymouth's No.3 bay platform. The original Southern main line between Plymouth and St.Budeaux was closed on 7th September 1964 and the train therefore remains on the Penzance main line for the first three miles before using the wartime connection between the SR and GWR, opened on 21st March 1941, to join the Southern route at St.Budeaux Victoria Road. The remnant of the main line as far as Bere Alston was singled on 7th September 1970 and one train working now applies from St.Budeaux; the single line staff, released remotely by Plymouth Panel, is obtained by the driver from the apparatus on the platform at Victoria Road station. The line passes twice under the Penzance line before descending to the east bank of the River Tamar. The view back to the left is dominated by the Royal Albert Bridge and Tamar Road Bridge and on the right is the one time rail-served armament depot.

After crossing Tamerton Lake the train passes the site of Tamerton Foliot station, closed on 10th September 1962, and onto the eight-span Tavy Bridge, which gives the railway such a dominant advantage over road transport on the Bere Alston peninsula. A sustained climb takes the train through Bere Ferrers where a local enthusiast has restored the station complete with a LSWR signalbox originally at Pinhoe and a collection of rolling stock in the former goods yard, and on through the lush rolling countryside of rural south-west Devon to Bere Alston, where the track ends abruptly just out of sight of the station platform.

When the line from St.Budeaux was singled all sidings except those at Ernesettle were removed. Bere Alston's layout was reduced to a single track running into the main platform and the connection with the line to Gunnislake was relocated to the Plymouth end of the platform to simplify train movements; the ground frame controlling the junction is worked by the guard and three minutes are allowed for the reversal. Chapter 8 continues the description of the line from Bere Alston, but it should be noted that most of the buildings, the island platform and signalbox survive, the latter as a permanent way cabin. After the main line north of Bere Alston closed a replacement bus service to Tavistock was operated by Sleep's until 1972; Western National displaced Sleep in the late 1980s and the link has been reinstated.

The line to Gunnislake is plain track and all loops and sidings have been removed. There is no staff at any of the stations and in the 1980s the station buildings at Calstock and Gunnislake were replaced by simple shelters. After many years of discussion Gunnislake station has been re-sited on the south side of the A390 road to allow removal of the railway bridge which had only 12 feet clearance for road traffic. The last train served the old station on 29th January 1994 and whilst the work to provide the new station was carried out services turned round at Calstock with a minibus connection to Gunnislake. The new station is on the site of the Perry, Spear & Co. coal depot but as the line was on a gradient of 1 in 40 the land had to be excavated, exposing arsenic and other remnants of the mining industry; this delayed matters and the train service was not resumed until 9th June 1994. Official opening of the new station, which includes a large car park and a turning area and bays for the seasonal connecting bus services, was on 23rd June 1994.

8 – The Route Described

Up train hauled by Ivatt 41323 at Chilsworthy on a May morning in 1964.

Before closure of the main line, branch trains used the outer face of the up island at Bere Alston platform. The station is similar to the others on the PDSWJ mainline, the principal buildings being of stone construction; there was a small goods yard and transfer sidings for branch traffic behind the Callington platform. On leaving the station the line immediately drops steeply at 1 in 39, curving sharply to the right. Shortly the line enters the Tamar Valley, and a splendid view downstream can be obtained. After passing through a short cutting the line swings sharply left to cross the valley on the imposing viaduct which does much to enhance the attractions of Calstock; looking downstream the remains of Calstock Quay can be seen below, and in the distance the course of the narrow gauge incline can be traced. A short distance upstream one of the last of the Tamar ferries operated, although much of its trade disappeared with the opening of the BAC.

The line has now entered Cornwall; Calstock station is situated at the end of the viaduct, on a sharp right angled curve (1 mile 55 chains). Although it was a crossing station, there was only one platform on the up side. The station buildings were of corrugated iron construction, and of a simple design used by Col Stephens on a number of lines. There was a water column at the end of the platform, and most trains took water here. On leaving the station the line starts climbing at 1 in 38 between the many market gardens clinging to the steep hillside, and shortly passes the remains of Okel Tor Mine, the first of many whose ivy covered chimneys are a common feature of the local scene. This section was extremely difficult for steam locomotives, the steep gradient starting at the platform end at Calstock, itself on a 7 chain curve, preventing any run at the bank. The branch left Bere Alston in a south westerly direction, but is here heading almost north east and across the river the main line can be seen high up on the hillside. However, the branch soon doubles back on itself on a curve of only 10 chains radius through a rock cutting and woodland—the curve is so sharp that in the days of steam it was possible to see the train engine from the first coach.

Beyond Calstock Church, set high above the village, the countryside opens out and to the left the old main line is visible once again, while ahead the branch can be seen near Gunnislake station, with Kit Hill in the far distance. The line is now running in a westerly direction alongside the Calstock-Albaston road past an ungated level crossing over which road traffic is protected by continental type warning signs. Trains now have to stop before proceeding cautiously over the ungated crossings. Shortly afterwards it is possible to catch a glimpse to the left of the disused Incline station of the ECMR; the buildings of which are used by a local farmer. and a short distance beyond the track bed of the abandoned portion of the ECMR joins the present line. At the approach to Gunnislake station a facing siding diverged on the down side to serve the coal depot of Perry. Spear & Co. Ltd (4 miles 35 chains).

Gunnislake station (4 miles 48 chains) boasted an island platform approached by a short subway under the down line. The station building was similar to but larger than that at Calstock. The station is about a mile from the village and is several hundred feet higher. In just under three miles from Calstock the line has climbed about 350 feet, much of the way on a gradient of 1 in 38. On leaving Gunnislake the site of Sand Hill Park Siding (4 miles 63 chains) was passed on the down side, and on the up side the remains of several mines, and sidings, can be seen. The gradient was slightly less steep, varying between 1 in 45-88, past Chilsworthy (5 miles 31 chains), a small halt on the up side. From the platform there was a magnificent view across the Tamar Valley, with far below the river winding through Blanchdown Wood. Beyond Chilsworthy, the line continued to climb past the large Hingston Down Quarries, the only ones still working in the area. The quarries were served by Whiterocks Siding (6 miles 2 chains) which rose steeply on the down side. The siding could only be served by up trains and incoming traffic was worked via Hingston Down Sidings (6 miles 21 chains). When traffic was heavy, down freights were divided at Gunnislake and one portion was taken to Hingston Down Siding, where it was reversed. The train then ran to Whiterocks Siding and shunted there as required before returning to Gunnislake. The train then left for Callington. Less than a quartermile beyond Hingston Down Sidings was Latchley, a small halt with a corrugated iron shelter on the down side (6 miles 39 chains). There was once a siding on the up side, adjacent to the loading platform of the former ECMR Cox's Park Depot. Beside the ungated level crossing was the ECMR station house. The small village is over a mile distant and lies some 500 feet below the station site.

Beyond Latchley there was a short descent at 1 in 150/200 and a longer stretch at 1 in 1000, followed by a half-mile climb at gradients between 1 in 200/54/143 past a derelict platform marking the site of Seven Stones Halt to the summit of the line nearly 700 feet above sea level. The line then levelled out before descending at 1 in 175 to Luckett station (7 miles 58 chains). The station buildings were of corrugated iron construction similar to those at Calstock. There was a goods loop, unlocked by a key on the electric tablet. Adjoining the loop was a loading bank, on which stood the station house of the ECMR Monks Corner Depot. From the platform Latchley station could be seen on the distant hillside. The line now ran along the flanks of Kit Hill, and three-quarters of a mile beyond Luckett was the site of Kit Hill Sidings, whence a narrow gauge inclined tramway ran up to the quarries on the hillside. The Gunnislake to Kelly Bray road ran beside the line for the remainder of the journey, which was on a falling gradient varying between 1 in 49/270. To the north a wide panorama across North Cornwall and West Devon came into view, and shortly the line negotiated a final sharp right-handed curve to arrive at Callington terminus (9 miles 50 chains). There was one platform partially roofed over; the station buildings were constructed from the ubiquitous corrugated iron. Originally the overall roof of the station extended across the adjoining track to form a carriage shed. The runround loop was outside the station and it was necessary for a train to back out of the platform before the engine could run round. There was a two road engine shed of wooden construction, which latterly housed two engines subshedded from Plymouth (Friary). One was stabled inside the shed and the other outside on the same road, the second road being occupied by loco coal wagons. The station platform was extended by the SR in 1927; this meant that the yard had to be remodelled and there was no longer access to the engine shed from the west end. The corrugated iron goods shed and several foodstuffs stores were situated on the up side, and on the down side sidings served the coal merchants' yards. From the station the chimney surmounting Kit Hill that forms the local landmark for miles around was clearly visible.

The branch was single track throughout, with crossing places at Calstock and Gunnislake, but as there was only one platform at Calstock two passenger trains could not cross there. There was an overall maximum speed limit of 25mph and several more severe restrictions of 5, 10 and 15mph. The staff and ticket system was used between Bere Alston and Calstock, and electric token between Calstock and Gunnislake and also between Gunnislake and Callington. By 1961 most of the signals were standard SR upper quadrants on rail built posts, but two lower quadrants survived at Calstock, and one at Gunnislake. There were no signal boxes, points and signals being controlled from small ground frames. Block instruments were housed in the station buildings.

Latchley with the 10.50am Bere Alston to Callington, 28 June 1956.

Luckett in 1962.

3.15pm from Bere Alston arriving at Callington behind 30192. 27 June 1956.

9 – Locomotives

Compared with its contemporaries amongst minor railways in the British Isles, the Callington line as a standard gauge railway has had a remarkably straightforward locomotive history. Other than the regauged mechanical curiosity inherited from the ECMR, all its locomotives were of standard design purchased new from the makers and suffered no major rebuilding throughout their lives.

However, it is with the little Neilson engine that we start as even for a locomotive in Colonel Stephens' flock, she had a varied career. She was one of a pair of 3ft 6in gauge 0-4-0ST's built by Neilson & Co. of Glasgow in 1871 (works Nos. 1660/1) for the opening of the ECMR. In appearance they were pure Neilson with that firm's characteristic "ogee" saddle tank and stove-pipe chimney. Apparently they soldiered on happily from the time of delivery to the time of their acquisition by the PD & SWJR and underwent no structural alterations during this period. Both engines became the property of the standard gauge company but it was not until the reconstructed line was nearing completion that they became redundant as narrow gauge engines. By this time No. 1 was in poor condition and was withdrawn in 1907 being sold in 1911.

This left No. 2 whose continued existence as a narrow gauge engine after the opening of the line through to Callington on the standard gauge must have caused the directors much headscratching. What to do with her? Sell? Scrap? In the event someone came up with the rather desperate idea of performing a conversion to standard gauge to make a station pilot for Callington or even a standby goods engine, when "A. S. Harris" was out of traffic. In fact, the regauging was carried out quite neatly in the shops at Callington under the supervision of H. E. Kemp, Locomotive Superintendent. Vacuum brakes, a pair of solid-centred trailing wheels and a new cab were fitted, whilst the motion and cylinders remained unaltered. However, alongside the railway's much larger standard gauge locomotives and rolling stock she always had something of the appearance of a clockwork mouse, in addition to which her haulage powers on the sharp gradients of the line were a great disappointment to her operators, so after four years of spasmodic activity she was sold in July 1912 to Colonel Stephens' eccentric Selsey Tramway, for the princely sum of £250 less carriage, and there she was to finish her days. However, before her demise she was rebuilt yet again using parts from the defunct Selsey 0-4-2ST "Chichester"—at the same time acquiring the name "Hesperus". Her appearance was now much altered due to a new higher-pitched boiler, frames extended at the rear and a larger cab. In this rather top-heavy condition "Hesperus" put in some good work on the near-level Selsey line until finally withdrawn and scrapped in 1927—but by then the writing was on the wall for the Selsey Tramway itself.

With their line nearing completion at the hands of the contractors, the PD&SWJR directors were naturally anxious to take delivery of their own locomotives and rolling stock, and in an effort to satisfy them, Hawthorn Leslie rushed the completion of the smallest engine, the 0-6-0 side tank, to deliver it to Bere Alston on 31st October 1907. Hawthorn's tender of £6,150 for the construction of the three locomotives was submitted in September 1906 and was approved by the Board of Directors on 10th October that year.

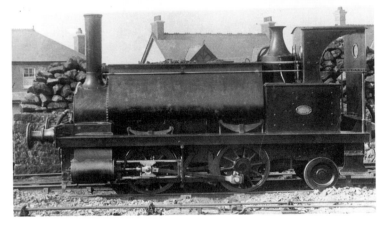

*Top: Neilson locomotive
in its original condition.*

*Left: Neilson locomotive
No 2 after conversion to
standard gauge.*

*Below: Builder's photo-
graph of* A. S. Harris
*carrying the incorrect
original lettering*

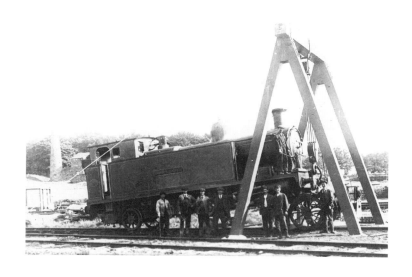

Top: Lord St Levan *under the sheerlegs at Callington.*

Right: The two Hawthorn Leslie 0-6-2 Tank Engines at Callington Earl of Mount Edgcumbe *in front.*, Lord St Levan *emerging from shed.*

Below: Lord St Levan *with passenger train at Bere Alston.*

Unfortunately in their hurry, the manufacturers mistook the name of the PD&SWJR director and applied the painted name "H. S. Harris" to the tank sides. However, the error was soon rectified when brass nameplates were cast carrying the correct name "A. S. Harris". The locomotive (works No. 2697) was a neat, compact outside cylindered design of unmistakable Hawthorn Leslie lineage and was intended as the PD&SWJR passenger engine. Upon arrival it was put to work on the construction of the line and numbered 3. When the railway was grouped into the LSWR in 1922, "A. S. Harris" was allocated the number 756 but never carried it as the South Western itself lost its identity in the following year and it was left to the Southern Railway to apply this number in 1923. Due to the limited number of classes permitted up the Callington line in early postgrouping years, "A. S. Harris" did not stray far from home until a draft of "O2s" arrived in 1929. The locomotive made an exceptional trip in 1928 when it was tried on the Wenford mineral line but found wanting, owing to inadequate coal and water capacity. However, Eastleigh works were happy to provide a home for the little engine as their pilot until 1931, when it was transferred to Nine Elms and thence gravitated to Stewarts Lane by nationalisation in 1948. This time the number 30756 was allocated but never carried as "A. S. Harris" was withdrawn on 27th October 1951 and scrapped at Eastleigh.

The directors were just as anxious to take delivery of their goods engines and, as a result, Hawthorn Leslie rose to the occasion and despatched "Earl of Mount Edgcumbe" and "Lord St Levan" on Boxing Day 1907—obviously some Christmas overtime was worked on Tyneside to get them ready. The locos carried their names on brass plates affixed to the tank sides and became PDSWJR Nos 4 and 5 respectively. In appearance they were enlarged versions of "A. S. Harris" though dimensionally they were considerably bigger and for their size were very powerful—their rated haulage capacity was greater than that of a 2MT tank—one feels that the railway directors must have been quite impressed with their namesakes. So satisfactory was the design that it was even proposed at a later date by the Southern to build two identical locos for the opening of the North Devon & Cornwall Junction line in 1925, and tenders for their construction were even obtained from Hawthorn Leslie & Co., but R. E. L. Maunsell produced his "E1/Rs" and the project was dropped.

Both locomotives passed to the Southern without carrying their LSWR numbers and it was left to the SR to inscribe them 757 and 758 respectively, though in a fit of post-grouping South Western enthusiasm, "Earl of Mount Edgcumbe" appeared inscribed "LSWR E757"! However, the local staff, who resented the change of ownership, soon rubbed the new lettering off the tank sides. Callington clung tenaciously to them until well into BR days despite infiltration by "O2s" and other classes and in 1955 they could be still found at Plymouth. But the end was in sight for the two old warriors and in 1957 they both went to Eastleigh – "Lord St Levan" to the scrapheap and the "Earl" for a final fling as shed pilot before it succumbed.

The livery of the PDSWJR's locomotives was initially blue—a similar hue to that used on locomotives on Colonel Stephens' other railways—but after the Colonel's departure from the Callington scene, his successor T. H. Gibbons recommended in 1912 that it would be more economical if the colour scheme were changed to South Western green "as this would wear better and be available cheaper from the SWR". One suspects the Colonel of having induced his erstwhile employers to buy a job lot of his blue paint of somewhat doubtful durability at an inflated price.

From time to time it was necessary to hire a replacement when a locomotive was stopped for heavy repair: the LSWR provided its Terrier tank No. 735 as substitute for

"A.S. Harris" *in* 1911 and O2 No. 226 following an accident to "Lord St Levan" in May 1918. Presumably the LSWR could not help at other times during the Great War because at various times the GWR loaned 0-6-0 saddle tanks Nos. 1946, 2020 and 2118 whilst Colonel Stephens came to the rescue in 1917 with "Walton Park", a Hudswell Clark 0-6-0 saddle tank originally built for the Weston, Clevedon & Portishead Light Railway, but which was by then being transferred from the Shropshire & Montgomeryshire to the East Kent Light Railway.

A. S. Harris *carrying Southern number but retaining LSWR lettering shortly after grouping.*

Parlous old age – A. S. Harris *at Stewarts Lane c.1948/9 in Southern livery but without its chimney!*

The end of the line – 1.0 p.m. to Bere Alston at Callington, August 1962.

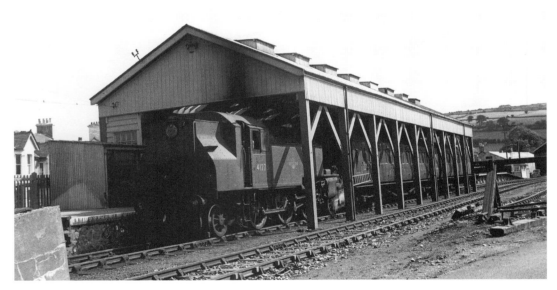

Callington station with the 10.40 a.m. from Bere Alston, August 1962.

10 – Intruders

When the Southern Railway took control after the grouping it appeared to be singularly unaware of the line's serpentine character, for it was proposed that all kind of unlikely classes of engines be used. Several classes of Adams 4-4-0 tender engine were permitted on the line, and it was envisaged that ex-LSWR "T1" and "O2" 0-4-4 tanks be used on freight work. It was even suggested that "A. S. Harris" could be replaced by a "B4" 0-4-0 dock tank.

The 4-4-0s did appear occasionally; "X2" No. 579 was rostered to work a six coach "Tamar Breweries" special from Devonport to Callington on August Bank Holiday Monday 1926. Doubtless the 7ft 1in driving wheels of 579 proved unsuitable for a similar train the following year was rostered for "T1" No. 73. In the next two summers a "T9" was specially authorised to work on the line but there is no record of their actually being employed and the through excursions were worked by "0395" class 0-6-0 goods engines in subsequent years.

On a journey up the line at any time between 1929 and the late 1950s, the motive power would almost certainly have been supplied by one of Adams' pretty little "O2s". These gallant little 0-4-4Ts, though considerably more advanced in years than the original PDSWJR engines, could put up excellent performances over the line's formidable gradients with scarcely lighter loads. In the postwar period there was normally one "O2" and one "757" on the line at one time. The "O2" was primarily for passengers and the "757" for goods duties though the rosters called for passenger and goods working by both. Regular performers were numbers 30183, 30192, 30216, 30225 and 30236: the latter engine being employed at Callington more or less continuously between 1953 and 1959. Their disappearance was sudden and complete—by 1961 they had been swept away by the Ivatt LMS-type 2-6-2Ts which had displaced the PDSWJR tanks in 1952 – capable engines to be sure, but sadly lacking that vintage charm of the "O2s". Amongst those engines of this class allocated to Callington shed at various times were 41275, 41315 and 41316, and they remained until displaced by diesels in 1964.

Among the other locomotive types employed were the "0395" class, used on both passenger and goods turns during the Plymouth blitz of the Second World War. In October 1941 the Southern inflicted the PDSWJR with an "E/1R" from Barnstaple to try to avoid double heading the heaviest trains, but the Callington men had the last laugh here for the converted Stroudley tank was in poor condition and soon went away in disgrace, having more than once stalled through lack of steam during its brief fortnight's sojourn. One may suspect the Callington men's natural bias in favour of their own engines, but it may well be argued that the Southern would have done better in 1927 to have perpetuated the Hawthorn Leslie design instead of the hybrid "E/1Rs", which only seemed really at home on the Torrington and Halwill line for which they were built, despite being tested over several of the SR's West Country branches.

When dieselisation took place in 1964 a D63xx class type 2 diesel hydraulic was used for goods and a railcar for passenger trains. The D63xx undertook passenger duties when more than one passenger train was required.

'Heritage' set unloads at tired old Gunnislake platform shortly before its resiting and rebuilding, a sad contrast to the smart layout pictured at the bottom of p26. A Western National Sundays only Okehampton bus waits for the orderly procession of transferring passengers.

The new Gunnislake station with car park and bus-turning area to right, July 1996.

11 – Operating the East Cornwall Mineral

The line commenced on Calstock Quay, about ⅛th mile east of the present viaduct. The original wharves had been considerably extended and improved by the company, and the management of the port taken over under the original Act. As altered, there was a continuous length of 1,359 feet alongside which barges and other river craft could be moored. At a point 500 feet short of the west end of the quay was the foot of the incline; this was single track, 35 chains long, on a gradient of 1 in 6, with a passing loop at the midway point. The working was by counterbalance, assisted by a small 14hp stationary engine. The maximum load permitted was two full wagons, or their equivalent, three empties. The working of the incline was entirely under the direction of the stationary engineman, and he was held responsible for equating, as far as possible, the ascending and descending loads. The actual work of securing the wagons to the wire rope was performed by the "signalman" at the upper end and "coupling man" at the quay. Wagons were attached to the rope by their centre coupling and side chains. Communication between the top and bottom of the incline was by means of electric bells, a complicated code of rings covering every contingency. This was later replaced by a telephone.

The half way loop was manned by a "signal boy" whose duties were laid down in very precise terms:

> "The Signal Boy stationed at the centre of the incline must pay particular attention to the wire rope, pulleys, rollers, points, etc., and wagons passing up or down, and should anything go wrong, he must immediately signify the same by putting his Semaphore Signal at Danger, and by raising and violently waving his Red flag to the Signalman at the top of the incline, who in his turn, will, in the manner last described, signal to the Engineman to stop hauling. Should these signals by any means be unobserved, attention must be attracted by shouting or any other available method."

The semaphore signal was situated on the west side of the line just above the upper end of the loop. As the incline was curved it could not be seen from the quay. The incline was not worked during the hours of darkness or in fog or falling snow.

Protection at Incline Station was afforded by "choke blocks" across the rails, and locomotives were prohibited from approaching within 40 feet of them. Shunting was entirely suspended when the "choke blocks" were open. Only one major accident ever occurred; this was due to the failure of the signalman at Incline to secure two trucks of granite correctly. Consequently they ran away, causing damage estimated at £93 9s 10d.

At the Incline Station there were the engine winding house, the engine shed, and sidings for marshalling the trains. Both engines were used on the upper section, all shunting on Calstock Quay being performed by horses. Beyond Incline Station the line continued to rise steadily for a mile to Drakewalls where a small public depot (now Gunnislake station) was provided for handling coal and agricultural produce. There was also a siding serving the ancient Drakewalls tin mine. A quarter of a mile beyond Drakewalls, the West of England Siding served the large Pearson's Quarry below and to the east of the line. Other sidings served the Plymouth Works, and Gunnislake Clitters Mine was connected to the

ECMR by an inclined tramway. The other intermediate public depots were at Cox's Park (Latchley), and Monks Corner (Luckett). There were several sidings serving the various tin; copper and arsenic mines, and quarries, the most important being those serving Hingston Down and Kit Hill Quarries.

The single line between Incline Station and Kelly Bray was worked on the time interval system, combined with single needle telegraph. A crossing loop was provided at Cox's Park, and it was also possible for two trains to pass at West of England Siding. As there was no agent at the siding, written orders were issued to each driver not to leave the siding until the arrival of the train travelling in the opposite direction. Trains proceeding towards Kelly Bray were designated up, and those towards Calstock down. A speed limit of 16mph was in force over the whole line. Because of the steep gradients, with a heavy train it was the practice in either direction to take half the train to Monks Corner, and return for the other half, and then work the combined train to Incline or Kelly Bray.

In addition to the incline signal, semaphores were provided at Cox's Park, Monks Corner and Kelly Bray. These were of the then customary two-wire pattern, showing all-right (arm lowered into post or white light), caution (arm raised half way or green light) and danger (arm horizontal or red light). Distant and home signals were provided, but they were not worked except when both engines were in steam at the same time. There were seven public road level crossings, four being manned by gatekeepers. Except at Cox's Park Depot, where the railway crossed a major road, the gates were kept closed across the highway and only opened to allow vehicles to cross. None of the crossings were protected by signals, and no lights were allowed to be shown in the direction of the railway from windows of the gatekeeper's houses between sunset and sunrise.

Although they were abandoned ninety years ago, the buildings at Incline station are still intact, and the course of the abandoned railway can be clearly seen.

Two plank open wagon seen on Kit Hill narrow gauge siding in 1937.

APPENDIX 1
PRINCIPAL DIMENSIONS OF LOCOMOTIVES

ECMR 0-4-0 tanks

	As built	No. 2 (Works No. 1661) rebuilt
Cylinders (outside)	10ins x 18ins	10½ins x 18ins
Coupled wheels	3ft lins	3ft lins
Coupled whelbase	5ft	5ft
Trailing wheels	——	1ft 9ins
Total wheelbase	——	9ft 4ins
Heating Surface	597 sq. ft	674 sq. ft
Boiler Pressure	85 lb	115 lb
Weight in working order	11 ton 15 cwt.	17 ton 5 cwt

PDSWJR tank engines

	0-6-2T	0-6-0T
Cylinders (outside)	16ins x 24ins	14ins x 22ins
Coupled wheels	4ft 0ins	3ft 10ins
Coupled wheelbase	11ft 0ins	10ft 6ins
Total wheelbase	16ft 9ins	10ft6ins
Radial wheels	3ft 0ins	——
Heating Surface	1,017 sq ft	697 sq ft
Boiler Pressure	170lb	170lb
Grate area	16½ sq ft	11 sq ft
Tractive effort	18,495 lbs	13,345 lbs

	t.	c.		t.	c.
Weight in working order	12	3		11	5
	14	1		13	0
	13	16		11	10
	7	3		—	—
	47	3		35	15

APPENDIX 2
LOADS OF TRAINS

In SR days passenger trains were restricted in load as follows

	number of non-corridor bogie coaches	
	1924	1934
'0415', '0298', '756'	4	3*
'O2', 'T3', 'X2', 'X6'	5	4*
'T9', 'T6'	6	—
'0395', '757'	6 and van	5†

* plus 1 PLV in fine rail and weather conditions.
† six in favourable rail and weather conditions..

Permitted number of loaded wagons

Section	Class of engine		
	757 & El/R	O2	0395 & 2MT
Calstock—Bere Alston } Calstock—Gunnislake }	14	10	12
Gunnislake—Hingston Down	18	12	18
Hingston Down—Callington	30	18	30
Callington—Calstock } Bere Alston—Calstock }	20	12	20

All classes of SR locomotives were prohibited on the branch except 'B4', 'El/R', 'C14', 'O2', 'T3', 'T6', 'X2', 'X6', '700', '735', '756', '757', '0415', '0298', '0395'. BR Standard and LMS class 2, 2-6-2 tanks were also permitted.

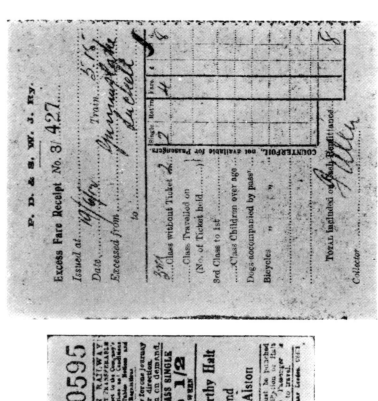

PDSWJR cheap ticket poster, Excess fare receipt and Southern Railway ticket issued on the train by the guard.

PASSENGER TIMETABLES

2nd March 1908 until further notice

Weekdays only

BERE ALSTON	8.33	12.00	2 55	6 05	7 40
CALSTOCK	8.40	12.07	3.02	6.12	7.47
GUNNISLAKE	8 55	12 21	3 16	6 26	8 01
LATCHLEY	9.08	12.31			8.11
STOKE CLIMSLAND	9 16	12 37	3.30		8.17
CALLINGTON ROAD	9 25	12 45	3 38		8 25

CALLINGTON ROAD	7.23	9.50	1.40	4.55	
STOKE CLIMSLAND	7.32	9.57	1.47	5.02	
LATCHLEY	7 39	10.03		5.08	
GUNNISLAKE	7.51	10.13	2.00	5.17	6.40
CALSTOCK	8 08	10.28	2.13	5.30	6.53
BERE ALSTON	8.15	10.35	2.20	5.37	7.00

8th June 1914 to 30th September 1914 inclusive

Weekdays only

BERE ALSTON	8.35	11.36	2.15	5C15	5B53	7.37	9B05	10B00
CALSTOCK	8.43	11.44	2.23	5C22	6B00	7.45	9B10	10B08
GUNNISLAKE	8 56	11 56	2.35	5C34	6B12	7 57	AB	10B21
CHILSWORTHY	A	A	A	AC	AB	A	AB	AB
LATCHLEY	A	12.03	2.41	5C40	6B18	8.04	AB	10B28
SEVEN STONES†	A	A	A	AC	AB	A	9B20	AB
LUCKETT	9 09	12.08	2.47	5C46	6B23	8.08	9B32	10B32
CALLINGTON	9 14	12 13	2 52	5C52	6B29	8 14	9B40	10B37

CALLINGTON	7.30	10.02	1.10	4.15	6.41
LUCKETT	7 36	10.08	1.15	4.20	6.46
SEVEN STONES†	A	A	A	A	A
LATCHLEY	7.41	A	1.20	4.25	6.50
CHILSWORTHY	A	A	A	A	A
GUNNISLAKE	7.47	10.17	1.25	4.32	6.56
CALSTOCK	7 59	10 29	1.37	4.44	7.08
BERE ALSTON	8 07	10 37	1 45	4.50	7.15

A Calls by signal to pick up or set down passengers
B Saturdays only
C Saturdays excepted.
† Trains only stop for Excursion parties by arrangement.

PASSENGER AND FREIGHT TIMETABLES

17th July 1932 until further notice

Weekdays

		Pass	Freight	Q Stone	Pass B	SX Freight	SO Pass	WThSO Pass	SO Q Freight	Pass	Pass	Pass	WThSO Pass D
BERE ALSTON	d	8.15	9.32	10.35	10.48	12.40	12.57	2.10		3.20	5.22	7.10	10.05
CALSTOCK	a	8.21	9.41	10.43	10.54	12.50	1.03	2.16		3.26	5.28	7.16	10.11
CALSTOCK	d	8.24	9.44		10.57	1.00	1.04	2.18		3.28	5.30	7.18	10.13
GUNNISLAKE	a	8.36	9.59		11.09	1.16	1.16	2.30		3.40	5.42	7.30	10.25
GUNNISLAKE	d	8X39	10X09		11X10	1X40	1X19		3.07	3.41	5.43	7.31	10.26
SAND HILL PARK SIDING						C							
GREEN HILL SIDING						C							
CHILSWORTHY	a	8.43			11.14		1.23			3.45	5.47	7.35	10.30
CHILSWORTHY	d	8.44			11.15		1.24			3.46	5.48	7.36	10.31
HINGSTON DOWN SIDING			10.19			C							
LATCHLEY	a	8.48			11.19		1.28			3.50	5.52	7.40	10.35
LATCHLEY	d	8.49			11.20		1.29			3.51	5.53	7.41	10.36
LUCKETT	a	8.53			11.24		1.33			3.55	5.57	7.45	10.40
LUCKETT	d	8.54			11.25		1.34			3.56	5.58	7.46	10.41
KIT HILL SIDING						C							
CALLINGTON	a	9.00			11.31	2.18	1.40		3.35	4.02	6.04	7.52	10.47

		Pass	Freight	Pass	Q Stone	Freight	Pass	WThSO Pass	SO Q Engine	Pass	Pass	WThSO Pass D
CALLINGTON	d	7.13	7.40	9.47			12.57		2.36	4.23	6.20	9.05
KIT HILL SIDING			C									
LUCKETT	a	7.19		9.53			1.03			4.29	6.26	9.11
LUCKETT	d	7.20	C	9.54			1.04			4.30	6.27	9.12
LATCHLEY	a	7.24		9.58			1.08			4.34	6.31	9.16
LATCHLEY	d	7.25	C	9.59			1.09			4.35	6.32	9.17
HINGSTON DOWN SIDING			C			10.29						
WHITEROCKS SIDING			C			10.31						
CHILSWORTHY	a	7.29		10.03			1.13			4.39	6.36	9.21
CHILSWORTHY	d	7.30		10.04		11.00	1.14			4.40	6.37	9.22
GUNNISLAKE	a	7.33	8.35	10.07		11.06	1.17	2.35	2.53	4.43	6.40	9.25
GUNNISLAKE	d	7.34	8X48	10X09		11X30	1X18			4.44	6.41	9.26
PERRY SPEAR & CO SIDING			C			11.37						
CALSTOCK	a	7.48	9.00	10.21	11.05	11.52	1.30	2.47		4.56	6.53	9.38
CALSTOCK	d	7.50	9.10	10.23		12.02	1.31	2.48		4.58	6.54	9.39
BERE ALSTON	a	7.57	9.19	10.30	11.14	12.11	1.38	2.55		5.05	7.01	9.46

48

PASSENGER AND FREIGHT TIMETABLES

17th July 1932 until further notice (continued)

Sundays

		Pass	Pass	Pass E	Pass	Pass
BERE ALSTON	d	9.22	12.25	3.00	7.15	9.32
CALSTOCK	a	9.28	12.31	3.06	7.21	9.38
CALSTOCK	d	9.30	12.34	3.08	7.22	9.39
GUNNISLAKE	a	9.42	12.46	3.20	7.34	9.51
GUNNISLAKE	d	9.43	12.47	3.21	7.35	9.52
SAND HILL PARK SIDING						
GREEN HILL SIDING						
CHILSWORTHY	a	9.47	12.50	3.25	7.39	9.56
CHILSWORTHY	d	9.48	12.51	3.26	7.40	9.57
HINGSTON DOWN SIDING						
LATCHLEY	a	9.52	12.55	3.30	7.44	10.01
LATCHLEY	d	9.53	12.56	3.31	7.45	10.02
LUCKETT	a	9.57	1.00	3.35	7.49	10.06
LUCKETT	d	9.58	1.01	3.36	7.50	10.07
KIT HILL SIDING						
CALLINGTON	a	10.04	1.07	3.42	7.56	10.13

		Pass	Pass	Pass E	Pass	Pass
CALLINGTON	d	8.23	11.30	2.08	6.15	8.30
KIT HILL SIDING						
LUCKETT	a	8.29	11.36	2.14	6.21	8.36
LUCKETT	d	8.30	11.37	2.15	6.22	8.37
LATCHLEY	a	8.34	11.41	2.19	6.26	8.41
LATCHLEY	d	8.35	11.41½	2.20	6.27	8.42
HINGSTON DOWN SIDING	a					
WHITEROCKS SIDING	d					
CHILSWORTHY	a	8.39	11.45½	2.24	6.31	8.46
CHILSWORTHY	d	8.40	11.46	2.25	6.32	8.47
GUNNISLAKE	a	8.43	11.49	2.28	6.35	8.50
GUNNISLAKE	d	8.44	11.50	2.29	6.36	8.51
PERRY SPEAR & CO SIDING						
CALSTOCK	a	8.56	12.02	2.41	6.48	9.03
CALSTOCK	d	8.58	12.04	2.43	6.50	9.05
BERE ALSTON	a	9.05	12.11	2.50	6.57	9.12

Notes:

- B — 18th July to 10th September departs Bere Alston 11.00am and runs 12 minutes later throughout
- C — Calls when required
- D — Will not run on Wednesdays from 14th September
- E — 17th July to 25th September only
- Q — Runs when required
- SO — Saturdays only
- SX — Saturdays excepted
- WThSO — Wednesdays, Thursdays & Saturdays only
- X — Cross train on single line

9th June 1958 until further notice

Weekdays

Station		Freight	Engine	Q Freight	Mixed	Engine	Pass	Freight	SX Freight A	SXQ Freight B	SO Mixed	WThSO Mixed	MTFO Freight Q
BERE ALSTON	d	6.20	8.03	8.03	8.24	9.03	10.40	11.13	12.40	12.40	1.02	1.58	2.10
CALSTOCK	a	6.29	8.09	8.11	8.30	9.09	10.46	11.21	12.50	12.50	1.08	2.04	2.19
CALSTOCK	d	6.34	8.11	8.13	8.33	9.12	10.49	11.24	1.00	1.00	1.09	2.06	
GUNNISLAKE	a	6.49	8.23		8.45	9.22	11.01	11.36	1.16	1.16	1.21	2.18	
GUNNISLAKE	d				8.49		11X04		1X45	1X40	1X25		
SAND HILL PARK SIDING	a		8.24	8.25						1.42			
SAND HILL PARK SIDING	d									1.52			
CHILSWORTHY	a				8.53		11.08				1.29		
CHILSWORTHY	d				8.53½		11.08½				1.30		
HINGSTON DOWN SIDING	a								1.55	2.00			
HINGSTON DOWN SIDING	d									2.15			
LATCHLEY	a				8.57½		11.12½				1.34		
LATCHLEY	d				8.58		11.13				1.35		
LUCKETT	a				9.02		11.17			2.22	1.39		
LUCKETT	d				9.03		11.18			2.32	1.40		
CALLINGTON	a		8.39	8.45	9.09		11.24			2.38	1.46		

Station		Pass	Pass	Pass	Freight	Pass	Freight	Freight	Freight	Pass	WThSo Mixed	SX Freight A	WThSO Mixed	Pass
			Through coaches to Plymouth Friary										MTFO Freight Q	
CALLINGTON	d	5.30		7.16		9.43	10.15			1.00				4.23
LUCKETT	a	5.36		7.22		9.49	10.22			1.06				4.29
LUCKETT	d	5.36½		7.23		9.50	10.27			1.07				4.29½
LATCHLEY	a	5.40		7.27		9.54				1.11				4.33½
LATCHLEY	d	5.41		7.28		9.55				1.12				4.34
HINGSTON DOWN SIDING	a						10.33					2.10		
HINGSTON DOWN SIDING	d						10.39					2.12		
WHITEROCKS SIDING	a						10.41					2.32		
WHITEROCKS SIDING	d						10.57							
CHILSWORTHY	a	5.45½		7.32		9.59				1.16				4.38
CHILSWORTHY	d	5.46		7.33		10.00				1.17				4.39
GUNNISLAKE	a	5.49		7.36		10.03	11.02			1.20		2.38		4.42
GUNNISLAKE	d	5.50	7.08	7.38	9.36	10.05	11X38			1X22	2.26			4.43
PERRY SPEAR & CO SIDING	a													
PERRY SPEAR & CO SIDING	d													
CALSTOCK	a	6.03	7.20	7.50	9.53	10.17	11.55	12.03	12.24	1.34	2.38		2.45	4.55
CALSTOCK	d	6.10	7.22	7.52	9.58	10.19	12.02	12.04	12.27	1.35	2.40		2.54	4.59
BERE ALSTON	a	6.20	7.29	7.59	10.07	10.26	12.11	12.09	12.36	1.42	2.47			5.0…

9th June 1958 until further notice (continued)

Weekdays cont

Down trains

Station		SX Freight (A)	Pass (C)	SO Pass (D)	Pass	SX Pass	Pass	SX Pass	SO Pass	Sundays — Q Freight	Mixed	Pass	Pass	Pass
BERE ALSTON	d		3.15	3.22	5.23	6.01	7.10	8.00	10.05		9.18	12.27	7.21	10.02
CALSTOCK	a		3.21	3.28	5.29	6.07	7.16	8.06	10.11		9.24	12.33	7.27	10.08
GUNNISLAKE	a		3.23	3.30	5.31	6.09	7X18	8.08	10.13		9.26	12.35	7.29	10.10
GUNNISLAKE	d		3.35	3.42	5.43	6.21	7.30	8.20	10.25		9.38	12.47	7.41	10.22
SAND HILL PARK SIDING	d	2.53	3.36	3.43	5.44		7.32	8.21	10.28	10.45	9.39	12.48	7.42	10.23
CHILSWORTHY	a		3.40	3.47	5.48		7.36	8.25	10.32		9.43	12.52	7.46	10.27
HINGSTON DOWN SIDING	d	3.03 / 3.08	3.41	3.48	5.49		7.37	8.26	10.33		9.44	12.53	7.46½	10.28
LATCHLEY	a		3.45	3.52	5.53		7.41	8.30	10.37		9.48	12.57	7.50½	10.32
LATCHLEY	d		3.46	3.53	5.54		7.42	8.31	10.38		9.49	12.58	7.51	10.33
LUCKETT	d	3.15	3.50	3.57	5.58		7.46	8.35	10.42		9.53	1.02	7.55	10.37
LUCKETT	a	3.20	3.51	3.58	5.59		7.47	8.36	10.43		9.54	1.03	7.56	10.38
CALLINGTON	a	3.27	3.57	4.04	6.05		7.53	8.42	10.49	11.05	10.00	1.09	8.02	10.44

Notes in columns: SX Pass (6.01) column — "5pm from Plymouth Friary"; Mixed column (Sand Hill Park Siding) — "Callington wagons only".

Up trains

Station		Pass	Engine	SO Pass	SX Freight	Sundays — Q Engine	Pass	Pass	Pass	Pass
CALLINGTON	d	6.20		9.10	9.15	10.15	8.15	11.12	6.30	9.10
LUCKETT	a	6.26		9.16			8.21	11.18	6.36	9.16
LUCKETT	d	6.27		9.17			8.22	11.19	6.37	9.17
LATCHLEY	a	6.31		9.21			8.26	11.23	6.41	9.21
LATCHLEY	d	6.32		9.22			8.27	11.24	6.41½	9.22
HINGSTON DOWN SIDING	a									
HINGSTON DOWN SIDING	d									
WHITEROCKS SIDING	a									
WHITEROCKS SIDING	d									
CHILSWORTHY	a	6.36		9.26			8.31	11.28	6.45½	9.26
CHILSWORTHY	d	6.37		9.27			8.32	11.29	6.46	9.27
GUNNISLAKE	a	6.40		9.30			8.35	11.32	6.49	9.30
GUNNISLAKE	d	6.41		9.33	9.36	10.30	8.36	11.37	6.50	9.31
PERRY SPEAR & CO SIDING	d				9.51					
CALSTOCK	a	6.53	7.09	9.45	10.08		8.48	11.49	7.02	9.43
CALSTOCK	d	6.54	7X20	9.46	10.11		8.50	11.51	7.03	9.44
BERE ALSTON	a	7.01	7.27	9.53	10.20		8.57	11.58	7.10	9.51

Note in Engine column (Gunnislake): "Work 8.00pm to Callington".

Notes

A	Not when 12.40Q Bere Alston runs
B	Runs when 1.45pm Gunnislake-Hingston Down Siding and 2.10pm Hingston Down Siding-Gunnislake not required
C	Will not run Saturdays 14th June to 13th September only
D	14th June to 13th September only
Q	Runs when required
MTFO	Mondays, Tuesdays & Fridays only
SO	Saturdays only
SX	Saturdays excepted
WThSO	Wednesdays, Thursdays & Saturdays only

APPENDIX 5
COACH SERVICE

Reprinted with permission from
Cyril Noall s "Cornish Mail and Stage Coaches" (Barton)

Another interesting four-coach service was begun in 1876 by the East Cornwall & South Western Coach Company Ltd, running from Tavistock through Gunnislake and Callington to Liskeard, and operated in conjunction with the London & South Western Railway. Under the heading "East Cornwall Coach scheme" a report in the "Cornish Times", 5th February 1876, stated that a largely attended meeting had been held at Golding's Hotel, Callington. Mr E. Nichollis and Mr W. S. Pearce of Tavistock described the company's aims, stated that as the South Western Railway was shortly to be extended to Tavistock the coach scheme had been promoted. Callington had hitherto been greatly neglected for want of railway accommodation and this would now be in a measure supplied by the coach.

The East Cornwall Coach's first run, under the auspices of the LSWR from Tavistock to Liskeard was reported in the same paper on 3rd June 1876. It was described as "a magnificent vehicle all but new, built for a member of the Four-in-Hand Club, regardless of cost, and it is the very perfection of style and convenience. It is likewise excellently horsed." The first passengers were the directors and several others interested in the venture. They had a good send off from the Bedford Hotel, and a considerable crowd assembled at Callington to welcome the coach. In less than the three hours allotted for the journey, the coach pulled up at Webb's Hotel, Liskeard where the passengers dined.

The East Cornwall Coach continued operating until about 1908 when Callington, Gunnislake and other stations were opened on the Bere Alston-Callington branch. The horses were changed at Golding's Hotel, Callington. A curious little time-table card issued by the proprietors gives some interesting particulars of its mode of operation.

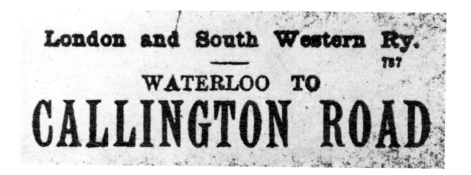

The GWR subsidised a horse bus service from Saltash to Callington to the tune of £156 per annum. On 1st June 1904 two GWR single deck 'Motor Cars' replaced the horse buses. Two Milnes Daimler vehicles dating from 1905 stand outside the 'car sheds' at Saltash.

Western National service 76 from Callington to Plymouth crosses the new Saltash bridge on its opening day 26th October 1961 presaging the demise of the railway at Callington.

STATION PLANS

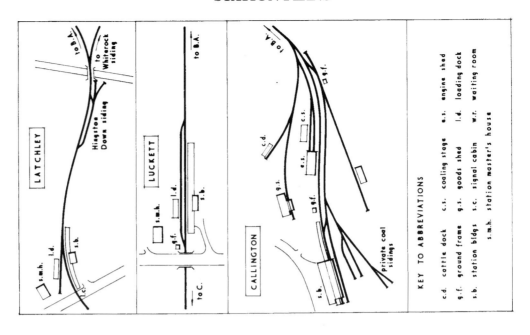

LATCHLEY

Hingston Down siding

to B.A.

to Whiterock siding

s.m.h. l.d. s.b. c.d.

LUCKETT

s.m.h. l.d. s.b. g.f.

to B.A.

to C.

CALLINGTON

to B.A.

g.f.

c.s.

e.s.

c.d.

g.s.

g.f.

s.b.

private coal sidings

KEY TO ABBREVIATIONS

c.d. cattle dock   c.s. coaling stage   e.s. engine shed
g.f. ground frame   g.s. goods shed   l.d. loading dock
s.b. station bldgs   s.c. signal cabin   w.r. waiting room
                         s.m.h. station master's house

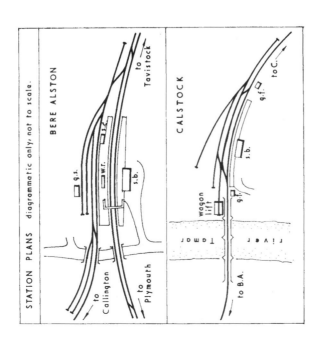

STATION PLANS diagrammatic only, not to scale.

BERE ALSTON

to Tavistock

g.s. w.r. s.c. s.b.

to Callington   to Plymouth

CALSTOCK

g.f.

s.b.

g.f.

wagon lift

river Tamar

to B.A.

to C.

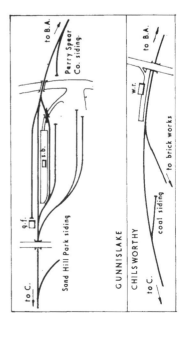

to B.A.

Parry Spear Co. siding.

s.b.

g.f.

to C.

Sand Hill Park siding

GUNNISLAKE

CHILSWORTHY

to B.A.

w.r.

to brick works

coal siding

to C.

54

Plymouth, Devonport and
South Western Junction Railway.

(Bere Alston & East Cornwall Line)

PARCELS RATES
REDUCTION.

The Public are respectfully informed that,
until further notice, the present Scale of
Parcels Rates to L. & S. W. and other Companies' Stations will be withdrawn, and a
universal Scale of Charges for through Parcels
traffic will be adopted.

Full particulars of these reduced charges
can be obtained from any Station.

All parcels should be consigned *via* L &S
W. R. and Bere Alston.

Traffic Office, Calstock,
JULY, 1908.

H. 516.   J. VENNING, PRINTER, CALLINGTON.

ACKNOWLEDGEMENTS

The authors have received ready assistance in the preparation of this account of the railways between Bere Alston, Calstock and Callington. The story is a fascinating one and they
hope that it will give as much pleasure in the reading as they obtained in the travel and
research which preceded the writing. Much of this research was done thirty years ago and
this means that some of the people and organisations whose help is acknowledged here are
no longer with us. Nevertheless, whether posthumously or not, they would like to record
their thanks in particular to C.R. Clinker for permission to use material originally published in "The Railway Magazine" in 1951; D. Bradley for supplying information about locomotives used on the line; R.L. Goodman of Launceston for assisting with material from the
"Cornish & Devon Post", and to the editor of that journal for permission to publish
extracts; the Archivist, British Railways Board, whose records are now in the Public Records
Office; D.B. Barton; Russell Bayles; W.E. Hayward; Michael Windeatt; the British Museum
and the Cornwall County Archivist.

Kind permission to use photographs has been given by:

J. H. Aston, p25, P26 (bottom), p31,
  p32 (bottom).
Russell Bayles, p7.
H. C. Casserley, p22 (bottom).
Roger Crombleholme, p26 (top),
  p32 (bottom).
Devon & Cornwall Rail Partnership,
  p40 (top).
English Electric Co. Ltd., p34 (bottom).
Grahame Farr, p8 (bottom).
Bryan Gibson, p2 (bottom).

Lens of Sutton, p19.
LCGB/Ken Nunn collection, p21
L & GRP, p16, p22 (top), p34
  (top and middle), p42.
John Scott Morgan, p37, p53 (top).
S. C. Nash, p56.
Douglas Stuckey, front cover (middle).
F. H. Casbourn, courtesy Stephenson
  Locomotive Society, p35 (bottom).
C. F. D. Whetmath, p13, p24, p38,
  p40 (bottom).

The maps on the inside covers and p43 are taken from the 6in to the mile, second edition
1907, with permission from the Ordnance Survey. The other maps and plans were specially
prepared by F. J. Mackett, A.R.I.B.A.

YESTERDAY . . . AND TOMORROW?

Devon County Council would like to re-open the main line from Bere Alston to Tavistock to relieve congestion on the roads into Plymouth whilst otheπrs think it feasible to reinstate the line throughout to replace the Great Western route from Plymouth to Exeter which is prone to storm damage along the sea wall at Teignmouth.

'T9' No. 30709 is climbing from Bere Alston to Tavistock with the Plymouth portion of the "Atlantic Coast Express" in June 1961, with the Tamar Valley and Calstock viaduct below on the right.